The Last Sweet Mile

The Last Sweet Mile

A Journey of Brothers

ALLEN LEVI

RABBIT ROOM
— P R E S S —

Published by
Rabbit Room Press
3321 Stephens Hill Lane
Cane Ridge, TN 37013
info@rabbitroom.com

ISBN: 978-0-9863818-1-2

Printed in the United States of America
2015
First Edition

To Dadbo and Mombo.
He adored you.

i look for the heroic.
i look for the momentous,
the glowing,
the breathtaking,
the things that make the ones who get remembered
get remembered.
i look for the feats that would command the attention,
turn the heads,
win the hearts,
of the masses that i believe need to know you,
the masses who would love you like i do,
if only they did.
The you that was,
the you now gone,
the never ending you.
i find them not,
but in their place
small and telling things.

Letter

DEAR FAMILY,

I have been a full-time, little-known singer/songwriter for eighteen years. As such, I have become accustomed to playing for small audiences and to writing songs that have very short shelf lives. I am an expert at working long hours to compose music that few, if any, will ever hear.

And yet it is an honor and a gift to be able to do the work I do. That anyone at all would listen astonishes me.

Perhaps those realities—the small audience, the challenge of words, the solitary hours, and the disruptive voice of futility (*Why throw your time away?* it asks)—all come into play as I begin this long letter to you.

Two Levis, seven Leikvolds (recently enlarged by a couple of Ritchies), six Ballengees (which includes a pair of Ziskas), seventeen Bizilias (with subsets of Railey, Willis, Kirkpatrick), and four Griffiths are the tiny audience I have in mind as I write these pages. Maybe, in years to come, there will be others, not yet born, who will take an interest in their ancestral history and find these recollections worthy of their time.

If they do, I can only hope that they will come away with some sense of how fortunate they are to be kin to the one that we each know and love as son, brother, uncle, cousin, and hero.

NEAR THE NORTHERN BORDER of Afghanistan, there is a city called Mazar-e-Sharif, a place most notable for the blue mosque that enshrines the body of Mohammed's son-in-law. It is a sacred site in the Muslim world.

In 2006, I moved to Mazar to teach English for the summer months. I had never been there before. And so, prior to making the trip, I studied the basics of Afghan history, watched some film, acquainted myself with the fundamental tenets of Islam, and followed current events in an effort to know about, understand, and pray for the country that had been home to my brother Gary for two years. Before going there, I would have told you I had a general sense of the place—its culture, its past, its deprivations and poverty—and that when I finally arrived in Mazar, it would feel somewhat familiar to me.

I was sorely mistaken.

Gary made the flight to Afghanistan with me—Atlanta to Paris, Paris to Istanbul, Istanbul to Kabul, Kabul to Mazar-e-Sharif. We celebrated my fiftieth birthday—pastries and espresso—one minute after midnight in the Istanbul airport while waiting for a delayed flight to our next destination.

When we arrived at Mazar, exhausted from the long day, and as we made the short drive from the airport to a neighborhood called Baba Kambar, I realized I had no vocabulary to describe what I was seeing. Ten minutes in the actual place was worth more than all the books or movies that could ever be written about it.

I—one who loves to distill experience into music and lyric—never wrote a song about Afghanistan. How does one write about that for which there are no adequate words?

ALL MY LIFE I have heard of how it hurts to lose a loved one—a spouse, a child, a sibling, a best friend. I have seen people endure the experience of terminal illness and have watched as their families dealt with the trauma of loss, some with remarkable finesse and others with awkwardness and anger. I have been moved, as we all have, by stories and movies and music that speak of the ultimate farewell.

And I've always known—of course I have—that death and dying are all around us all the time.

But amazingly, at fifty-six, I had never lost anyone close to me.

I would probably have told you, before Gary got sick, that I had some general sense of what loss and grief are all about and that when I finally got there, they would feel familiar to me.

Again, I was sorely mistaken.

The death of my brother was far more hurtful, and far more final, and far more beautiful, than I could ever have imagined.

I HESITATE, EVEN NOW, to attempt writing about Gary's life and the year of his illness. I am under no delusion that a few well-chosen words can begin to recreate, even in minuscule degree, the soul that was—*is*—my brother. It is beyond my power to write anything that can remotely recreate or capture the last year we spent together. But I feel obligated to try.

My only certainty as I begin these writings is that I shall fail, maybe miserably so, in expressing what I most want to say.

So why make the effort?

I am driven partly by compulsion, partly by duty, and partly by desperation: compulsion because I am convinced that Gary's life, humble though it was, needs to be memorialized in some permanent form in order that it might continue to challenge and encourage the rest of us; duty because I feel that while we all knew Gary in unique ways, no one knew him better than I did or can speak more comprehensively about his life than I can; desperation because, at less than two years after his passing, I can already tell that my memories of Gary— healthy *and* sick—are getting hazy. This opportunity to think so pointedly about his life, as bittersweet as the experience might prove to be, is a gift I welcome. And I have a suspicion that the time will come when, older and *more* forgetful and closer to my own end, I will return to these memories for hope and consolation. *If one so dear as Gary is on the other side,* I can imagine myself thinking, *I am glad that my reunion with him daily draws nearer.*

That said, I like to think that deeper than compulsion or duty or desperation, there is a love of brother for brother that is the truest motive for these pages.

At the outset, I recognize that my affection for Gary might very well impair my ability to write objectively about him, a risk that seems always present when one is describing one's hero. I don't wish for any of us to remember him as anything other than what he was—a man deeply flawed and conscious of it, but deeply forgiven and conscious of that too. Gary could be damnably bull-headed, frighteningly careless with his words, embarrassingly blunt, cussedly contentious, and at times a bit quick to wrath. He was, by his own admission, a full menu of human imperfection. But no one regretted that fact more than he did.

If I seem in these pages to overlook or understate Gary's bad side, it is not because I lack the necessary information. I intend to give his shortcomings the appropriate and proportionate attention that they deserve. In other words, not much.

In a spirit of full disclosure, and out of respect for the fact that there are many different opinions about Jesus and His followers, I should warn you that in these pages I will speak unreservedly about Gary's love for Christ. Among our family, as in others, there will probably always be some who are believers and some who are not. There will be some who are resolute in matters of faith and some who will struggle with questions and doubt. There will be some who are decidedly *for* and others decidedly *against* anything pertaining to the narrow way of Jesus.

Regardless of your perspective on matters of faith, I hope you will be able to remember and celebrate Gary's life as one that was full of charity, especially toward those who did not share his views concerning God and salvation. It can do us no harm, and may possibly do us good, whether we are Christian or not, to sit at the feet of one who lived and died with the unmitigated affection of so many.

Some of us knew Gary much better than others did. I like to think that all of us who knew him at all knew him well enough to agree that even if it was woefully imperfect, his love for Christ, which he expressed daily in his love for people everywhere, was *the* distinguishing motive of his life.

I could try, of course, to write about him without mentioning his faith. His résumé, after all, is impressive even if one doesn't know anything about his creed or theology. But to write of him in that way would not only be dishonest, it would be dishonoring. To describe him without reference to what was most important to him would amount to an act of fraud. In the process, I would have to create a straw man—a Gary none of us knew, a Gary who wasn't really Gary at all. My respect for him will not permit that degree of compromise. And so, at the risk of including things that might prove uncomfortable or off-putting to some, I will write without reservation of the only Gary I knew: a man who was laughter incarnate and kind beyond measure, a man who loved Christ, who had a deep reverence for Scripture, who was burdened for the souls of others, and who believed in life everlasting.

LET ME STATE THE obvious. This will be a long letter. And even though I am writing it specifically to you, my family, I recognize that it might eventually find its way into other hands. That, by the way, is not at all an unwelcome prospect; I would like very much to introduce others to Gary. If I seem on occasion to include information about him that is obvious to us, it is for the benefit of those who might be meeting him for the first time.

Regardless of what we call it—letter, book, portrait, memoir— this is not intended to be a biography of Gary's life. My failing memory, along with the fact that he lived so many of his adult years out of our view and in far away places, would make it impossible to compile anything like a biographical record. What I hope is that from reading these pages, you'll retain a clear recollection of who Gary was *essentially*, and you'll gain a better idea of the man he wanted to be and was indeed becoming.

I hope too that these pages might encourage conversations between us who were fortunate to be his family. I am sure that each of you has reminiscences of Gary's life and you could add your own colorful brushstrokes to the portrait I'm trying to paint. I would be delighted to receive *your* letter about him in the mail someday.

Throughout these pages, I'll be making reference to "the farm," a piece of land—about fifteen hundred acres comprising timber and pasture—that Dad and Mom purchased in 1968, just east of Hamilton, Georgia. It is where I have lived since 1992. It is a place where, over the decades, the extended family has gathered time and again for weekends, holidays, and special occasions.

As I write this, I am sitting on my front porch, facing north. Three hundred yards or so to my left, across the pasture and the pond, is Gary's house. Four hundred yards straight ahead, across the field, is "the big house," where Dad and Mom live.

Technically, this land is not a farm. We do not and never have row-cropped it nor grown animals for sale. Our crop, if we have such, is pine trees.

And beauty.

And memories.

In that regard, this is rich ground, steeped in the sacredness of small things. Gary's footsteps and fingerprints are thick around the place. As I sit here, thinking about him, I need only raise my eyes and look in any direction to see something that resurrects a picture of him in my mind. From a hundred tiny monuments all around this place, he still speaks.

I hope I can convey clearly what he says.

My fear of failure as I begin this letter almost keeps me from writing at all. My sense of failure when I finish will probably make me reluctant to share it with you. But I write these pages—emboldened by the love that Gary had for me and for us, and I for him and for you—trusting and prayerful that they will do us good somehow.

If you read to the final page, which I hope you will, I am confident that whether you agree with Gary on "ultimate things" or not, you will be grateful for his legacy and, even more so, that—as he did you—you will love him for the wonderful soul he was. He deserves more ink and better ink than I can give him, but these words are all I've got.

Button

IMAGINE A LITTLE BOY.

It is a Sunday morning, early 1960s, and true to the deep but increasingly fragile roots of Southern tradition, he is enduring the weekly ritual of getting ready for church. With a bit of help from his parents and in response to the credible threat of what might happen if he doesn't cooperate, he has put on his "good" clothes, though why they are called "good" is beyond his comprehension. The navy blue pants, the pressed white shirt, the polished shoes, the clip-on tie—those good clothes—will remain, at least for the next few minutes, possibly an hour or two, clean and unwrinkled, tucked in and ready for parental scrutiny. After that, all bets are off.

In a nod to high fashion, his mother has bought him and his slightly older brother straw fedoras to wear.

All the while, there is a dog in the yard, or a bike or a bug or a ball, that is on the busy mind of that little boy.

Someone tells him not to forget his coat, a plaid sport coat that, to his thinking, serves no purpose but discomfort and inconvenience. He hurriedly puts it on, contorting, as all men do, to get arms into the sleeves. He buttons it midway down the torso.

But he misaligns.

He puts the middle button in the top hole.

And he is happy to leave it that way.

Someone—an adult—says, "Okay, y'all stand together and look at the camera. And smile."

I HAVE AN OLD photograph, several actually, of the five children—Beth, myself, Gary, Linda, Laura—in front of our house on Roswell Lane in Columbus, Georgia.

The house is a split-level ranch style. There are small shrubs in front, maybe newly planted, behind us children. There is a dog named Bo to Gary's right.

It had to have been a Sunday morning. Why else would we all be so dressed up? And, sure enough, Gary's coat is buttoned in perfect misalignment either because he was in a little-boy hurry to get outside or, just as likely, because he didn't know any better. At that young age, five or six, his unassailable logic must have been that if the button fits the hole and the coat doesn't fall off, then it must be right.

I asked Mom to tell me something about his earliest years. She shared some of her memories with me but also told me that if I would go through old family pictures, I'd be struck—and amused—by how often Gary buttoned his coat the wrong way. She would know, of course, since she was the one who had to correct his miscalculations. There was something about that minute detail of Gary's childhood that seemed indicative to Mom of all he might ever be, though she could not put a word to it.

I'm not sure what the word is either.

Perhaps it was early evidence that Gary would be someone with a clear sense of priorities. Maybe it was one of his earliest declarations in life that there are some things that matter a lot and some things that don't.

Getting the buttons right was a "don't."

Dressing quickly, so that he could get on with the more serious business of boyhood—the dog at the door, the bug in the jar, the game in the yard—was a "do."

As he grew older, that sense of priority would sharpen and mature, and the things that mattered most to him would change for the better. But in some sense deep and true, Gary would never cease to be the boy in that picture, smiling and ready.

He would eventually learn to button his coat properly. But the sweetness of his countenance in those family photos—the kindness, the innocence, the gentleness, the mischief, and the twinkle—stayed with him. Till the end, he was all boy in the best sense of the word—curious, active, imaginative, engaged, playful, unchildishly childlike.

He was my brother.

My best friend.

My hero.

THAT LITTLE BOY WAS born on June 30, 1957, the son of a forester dad and a schoolteacher turned stay-at-home mom in Bay Minette, Alabama, near Mobile. When he was a year old, the family—at that time, a young hard-working couple with three babies, Beth (four years old), me (two), and himself (one)—moved to Georgia where Dad would build a successful timber business with childhood friend Noll Van Cleave. Linda and Laura were born in Columbus shortly after we moved there.

We, the five children, grew up in an era and in a locale that valued good manners, chores and allowances, PTA, free time in open spaces, unorganized sports, family meals daily at a supper table, saying grace, low technology, and respect for elders.

In the distant background of our lives—distant at least in the minds of us children—the chaos of Vietnam, assassinations, segregation, unrest, and anger tore at the bigger world in ways that, even now, are difficult to assess and interpret.

But the children of Roswell Lane—and there were lots of us: the Taylors, the Kents, the Smiths, the Jenkins, the Molnars, the Parkmans, the Fishers, the Mizes, the McGlamrys—were blessedly too young to appreciate the changes that were being contended for outside our stable, middle-class neighborhood. On Roswell Lane, we feared none of those momentous things.

What most of us did fear was "the rod" (a.k.a. the belt, the switch, the paddle, the stick), a commonly accepted and widely utilized tool for teaching children to do right and respect authority. "Spare the rod, spoil the child" was a precept that had considerable traction in our neighborhood, both at home and in the schools. I know the practice seems draconian to enlightened minds of the twenty-first century, but many of us who endured "whippin's" will attest to their effectiveness, their harmlessness, their strategic worth, and even to the affection that inspired them. They might or might not have been the best way to correct a child, but they were, in my estimation, certainly not the worst.

If whippings had been baseball cards, Gary would have amassed the most comprehensive collection of players known to man. Since Mom was usually the parent closest to the scene of our juvenile infractions, she was the chief disciplinarian at our house. She would tell you that chasing Gary down, and giving him spankings, was one of the main ways she stayed in shape as a young mother.

He was a lovingly mischievous kid, prone to finding trouble but not in a mean or defiant way. Trouble, better said, found him.

An angry neighbor once called to say that Gary had picked all of the flowers from her meticulously tended front yard. Mom already knew about the larceny. The flowers were in a vase in her kitchen. He had picked them for her.

Gary grew up in the public schools and finished his primary education in Columbus. As a boy, he struggled with dyslexia. He found schoolwork difficult and preferred, like most boys, the freedom of the outdoors to the confinement of a classroom. His reading improved, with help, and he managed, just barely, to pass all of his classes. He graduated high school in 1975, a well-liked and popular kid who had distinguished himself as a competitive runner and all-around good guy.

Gary went to college at Troy State University in Troy, Alabama, on a partial track scholarship, and a year later he transferred to Abraham Baldwin Agricultural College in Tifton, Georgia. In that salt-of-the-earth agricultural setting, he was among kindred spirits—hunters, fishers, farmers, cowboy types—who probably had little admiration for the bookish life. After a year or two there, he transferred to the University of Georgia in Athens, where he finally received his degree in agricultural economics in 1979. After Gary passed away, I found his diploma in the bottom of a cluttered file cabinet, an indication of the very small—button small—importance he attached to that particular accomplishment in his life. I am sure that it never crossed his mind to frame it and put it on display, though few diplomas were more a testament to tenacity and perseverance than his.

What was important, and did matter most of all to Gary, was that he had become a follower of Christ while a student at the University of Georgia.

After graduation, he went into the timber business with Dad and then, sometime in the mid-1980s, left the business world, attended seminary for a year at Columbia International University, and spent the rest of his life as a vocational Christian missionary.

By the time the little boy with the misaligned buttons passed away on July 22, 2012, he had the following accomplishments to his credit (I list them in no particular order, and the time periods are approximations):

He spent a year working with deaf children in Jamaica.

He lived for a year with a non-English-speaking Costa Rican family in San Jose so he could learn Spanish. He told me it was the hardest, loneliest year of his life—though he did eventually become fluent in Spanish.

He lived for six years in Spain, partly in Madrid, partly in Pola de Siero, doing evangelistic and church-planting work.

He lived for six months in the jungle of Peru beyond the reach of electricity or modernity, helping a small team of missionaries take the gospel to a tribe in a remote part of the rain forest.

He resided for two years in Bosnia shortly after cessation of the ethnic war of the 1990s, doing charity and evangelistic work in bombed-out Sarajevo.

He lived in Macedonia for two years and traveled into Kosovo during hostilities there.

He lived in Afghanistan off and on for five years, doing humanitarian and evangelistic work.

He smuggled Bibles into China.

He became a proficient paraglider, excelled in hobbies of cycling and turkey hunting and beekeeping, learned to snow ski while working on a cattle ranch in Colorado, and became skilled at turning wood on a lathe.

He wrote a book of devotionals.

He saw the bombed-out buddhas of Bamiyan, the tulip gardens of Keukenhoff, bushkazi in Afghanistan, bullfights in

Spain, Wimbledon in London, and some of the most famous art museums in the world.

He traveled on shorter trips to numerous countries, including Japan, Mali, Jordan, India, Ecuador, and Turkey.

He became a self-taught banjo player and saxophonist.

He loved to read.

He enjoyed chess.

He was an amateur magician.

He planted a thousand blueberry bushes just north of his house a couple of years before getting sick and had hopes of using them to generate income for ministry in the future.

He owned and operated a small tree nursery.

He enjoyed cooking and giving food away.

He was a skilled marksman.

He lived contentedly as a never-married single man.

He loved laughter and was able, like no one else I've ever known, to bring it out of others.

He was endlessly fascinated by the natural world and often took walks around the farm to become better acquainted with the creatures that were in his neighborhood.

In everything he did, and everywhere he looked, and in every endeavor he undertook, he saw the Kingdom of God.

He was the most interesting person I ever knew.

And the kindest.

HE WAS ALL THAT—a composite of interests, traits, and experiences. For each place he ever lived, there is a cast of characters and a host of stories to be told. For every stamp in his passport, I am certain there is a book's worth of material to be discovered. I wish now that I'd taken better notes of the time I spent with him. The reminiscences and stories that follow offer a glimpse, a mere flyover, of the life called Gary. We are like little boys trying to watch a ballgame through a hole in the outfield fence. What is visible to us is captivating, but we wish all the while that we could see more.

Call

Since 1997, I've used a small book of meditations—*A Diary of Private Prayer* by John Baillie—to guide me in my morning devotionals. For each day of the month, there are morning and evening selections printed on the right-hand pages of the book. On the left side are blank pages where if one wants to write down a need or record an occasion of thanksgiving, there is room to do so (as, for instance, when one hears the first whip-poor-will of springtime or has a good harvest of honey from his beehives).

Whenever I fill all of the left-hand pages of the book—it usually takes three or four years—I retire the copy and begin another.

In the copy I'm presently using, there is an entry dated June 21, 2011, which simply says, "Gary feeling down. Lord, give him encouragement, restore gladness and joy to him."

Sometime earlier that year, maybe even late 2010, Gary began to express concerns about being moody, irritable, and forgetful. He thought, without really knowing what it was or how it worked, that he might be experiencing depression. He knew something was out of sorts but had no idea what it was. He was in extremely good physical shape, was continuing his daily rigors of woodworking, was riding his bicycle on a regular basis, and for the most part maintained his good humor and *joie de vivre*. But as spring moved on, he would tell us—with concern but no urgency—that something wasn't quite right.

We noticed his tendency to be forgetful and repetitive but were not overly bothered by it. Those of us closest to him suspected that we too were suffering from the same tendency. And yet, when Gary continued to complain, our uneasiness grew. Mom was the first to be concerned; she noticed that he would ask a question—always "Where's Allen?"—over and over in a short span of hours.

By spring of 2011, Gary had been stateside for the better part of a year, after having made a couple trips of several months each to Afghanistan, and I wondered if maybe he was simply finding it difficult to be home without a regular job. On one occasion, he left the farm for several days and went to north Georgia for a time of prayer, thinking that his problem might be purely a matter of the soul.

Not long after that, in early summer, Gary took a trip to visit with friends in Ecuador. While he was there, he experienced extremely painful headaches, something he'd never had before. Shortly after that trip, he went to visit our sister Linda in Alabama. When he got there, he could not remember the names of his nephews, a lapse that made him, and us, realize he needed medical attention.

I am sure that before this point we had encouraged Gary—maybe even pestered him—to see a doctor. He had put it off on the assumption that if he could ride his bike thirty miles or more a day and manhandle hundred-pound blocks of wood on a lathe, he was physically healthy. The forgetfulness, though, frightened him and finally forced him into the doctor's office.

It had been so long since Gary had been to a doctor that he did not have one he could readily call. We were able to get him an appointment with a dear soul and beloved new friend of the Levi family named Harvey Harris. A complete physical was scheduled for a couple of days later, a Thursday in late July.

The results for all the tests were normal.

But, providentially, as Gary was leaving the doctor's office, he happened to see Janet Fluker, whom he had dated decades earlier. She knew Gary well and was working as a physician assistant in Dr. Harris's office. Gary told her why he had come in; we would learn later that after he left the office, Janet had asked Dr. Harris about the visit. They reviewed the test results together, confirmed that there was nothing to indicate cause for concern, and discussed whether Gary might indeed be depressed. Janet told the doctor that she knew Gary and his family very well, that she did not consider him a likely candidate for depression, and that she felt further testing was in order.

Later that evening, Gary got a call from the doctor's office, asking that he return the following day for a brain scan. The scan took place on Friday. They would call in a few days to report the results.

IT WAS A CLEAR, hot, midsummer Saturday morning, and I was working in my yard. Gary drove to my house in his truck to tell me he'd just gotten a call from Janet. She and Dr. Harris wanted to meet with him immediately. And there was the foreboding instruction that he should bring somebody with him.

For the first of many times that we would do so in months to come, Gary and I, never bashful about physical displays of brotherly affection, hugged and, rather inexplicably, cried together.

I think we both knew at that moment, without yet fully knowing, that life was about to change for us.

Years ago, I wrote a song that says: "Every day there is something / to remind me I am small."[1] It makes the obvious, but easily forgettable, point that we are frail, transient beings. The immensity of space, the incomprehensible miracle of the molecular world, the vagaries of economies, the depth of cruelties committed and powers abused all drive home the reality that any single life, against the backdrop of creation and history, is a microscopic ephemera. Wonderful too, yes. But microscopic.

Every day there is something to remind me I am small.

Cancer, I would learn, is one of those things.

We met with Dr. Harris and Janet at her home.

They told us Gary had a brain tumor. A stage four glioblastoma. A "glio." We had the usual questions as to the particulars—how long has it been there, how fast is it growing, is it operable, can it be treated and how—but the sobering reality about which there was no doubt was that my brother was very sick.

In a matter of minutes and with the pronouncement of a handful of words, life changed irreversibly for our family. Dying and death, which had previously been strangers to us, were suddenly squatters on the farm.

We left Janet's house, drove back to Hamilton, and told the news to Mom and Dad.

We called family.

We began to let friends know.

I'm not at all certain what I'd call the feeling I felt that day.

It was Afghanistan again. Unfamiliar territory.

There was heartache, fear, and powerlessness. There was love, gratitude, and tenderness. There was laser clarity, and there was the fog of not knowing. There was a profound sense of smallness but also—I almost hesitate to say it—a sense of joy and hope. The only things that ever should have mattered were the only things that did matter that day.

It was a feeling similar to what many of us might have experienced on 9/11: "When death was all around us / we were never more alive."[2]

What was conspicuously absent from the family that day, or the days that followed, was any sense of bravado. No one expressed fierce determination to get tough and "beat this thing." We knew that neither our attitude nor our faith, no matter how positive or resolute, would overcome mortality. From the start, I think we all understood that this might be Gary's time to die.

That might seem fatalistic. But please understand, we did not lose faith, ever, in the possibility that God might heal Gary of cancer, either miraculously or medically.

We never gave up that hope. But we did surrender.

Not to the disease, but to God.

We would trust Him.

Gary's own faith in Christ and his words of constant counsel grounded us from the start. We resigned ourselves to the goodness of God, asked God for healing, and prepared ourselves to serve Gary and one another as best we could.

We were on new ground. But we had promises carved on our souls. We had the imperfect but tenacious love of family. We had a community around us. We had stories and laughter and music.

It was day one of the best year of my life.

A MESSAGE TO FRIENDS, from July 24, 2011:

Some of you know that a group of men meet at my house every Thursday morning to pray, to study the Bible, and to organize for involvement in our community. That gathering, for all intents and purposes, has been my church life for the past twelve years or so since work as a musician requires me to be out of town on many or most weekends.

This year we are reading the Scripture cover to cover, our third time to do so. I have been struck on many occasions at how the day's reading was so perfectly timed for the day's circumstances, as if the text had somehow been scripted for a particular moment in my life.

This morning I read the familiar words of Romans 8, which tell me that nothing can separate me from the love of God, which is in Christ Jesus. They go on to say that God causes all things to work together for good to those who love Him. They explain that God's overarching purpose in our lives is to conform us to the likeness of Christ. They declare with comforting finality that God is "for us."

Those words are timely.

Yesterday, my brother Gary and I met with his doctor and were told that he (Gary) has a brain tumor about the size of a quarter, likely malignant, on the back-left side of his brain. Given that Gary is healthy and active, the news was more than a little surprising. At present, there are medical decisions to be made, plans that need to rearranged, questions that need to be asked and answered. On one level, we're thankful that the source of Gary's recent forgetfulness and headaches seems to have been identified, and we are hopeful that the tumor might be removed and followed up with chemo and radiation.

On another level, we are very afraid at the prospect of losing him.

Many of you have already gotten word of his condition and have written to express your concern and to let us know that you're praying. I need not tell you how grateful and encouraged we are by such kindness. Might I ask, if you *are* someone who prays, that you remember Gary to the Lord? I still don't understand, and probably never will, how prayer works, but I know that God tells us to do it, promises His attention if and when we do, and assures us that He'll not give stones to the child who asks for fish. For you who've already taken Gary's case to God, thank you. For those who will, you are in exceptionally good company. Thank you.

At the risk of sounding melodramatic, I can tell you that when I've not been crying in the last 24 hours, I've been an inch away from doing so. I realize it has taken decades, and the fertile soil of deep friendship, to grow these tears. They have waited a lifetime to be spilt and will not be denied. They remind me how rich I am to have the brother and full-time hero that Gary has been to me over the years. And I look forward to walking this next part of the path with him, grateful for those who will be alongside us, including those like you.

We will trust.

"God is for us."

Table

I'M SITTING ON MY porch on a clear morning. Across the pasture and the pond is Gary's house. It really should be a museum or something, a shrine to hospitality.

Gary's love for people—a thing always visible, expressive, winsome—was nowhere more manifest than in his habit of hospitality. His house radiated with life. It was a place of frequent gathering. How often have I looked across the field to see cars coming up the dirt road to his house, especially around suppertime? I always knew that whoever was in those cars was heading to an oasis, to a broad space of welcome and cheerfulness and healing.

I was often privileged to be a guest at those gatherings.

Gary believed that one of the most under-enjoyed gifts in life, and one of the most underutilized resources of the American church, was the American house—the meal table in particular. I can think of many ways to describe his small kitchen, but "underutilized" is not one of them. Gary's line of reasoning seemed to be that if God had seen fit to give him a house, then he would use it to share God's love and do God's work. And use it he did. Friends, family, neighbors, married couples, people in distress, missionaries, high school and college kids—they all left their footprints on the heart-pine floors of his modest abode, a house that consisted, in addition to the kitchen, of an open dining room and sitting area with a small fireplace and vaulted ceiling, lots of windows, one bathroom, a bedroom and a half, and a porch with a view. The stories that were shared in that place, the laughter set free, the topics discussed, the good-natured disagreements, and the questions pondered would fill volumes. I have no doubt that lives were enriched, challenged, and changed forever under the roof of that house. Guests have told me so.

Those evenings usually unfolded something like this: greetings and small talk would be exchanged, folks would gather at the table, food would be set out, and a spoken prayer would be said. That prayer was usually a short offering of thanks for the day, for the guests, for the meal, and for the gospel.

Eating began. Conversation continued.

Gary's table—a heavy oak piece that Mom and Dad had bought early in their marriage—seated six comfortably. If eight or ten were present, as was often the case, everybody squeezed in. No one seemed to mind.

The plates and dishes he used were not fancy or delicate. They did not always go together. Silverware and drinking glasses were often a mongrel assortment, especially if the number of guests exceeded his supply of matched place settings. Chairs were also assorted.

Almost always, there was a flower in the center of the table—a blossom, a sprig or bough of something green, usually taken from the vicinity of his house.

Gary did not expect nor fish for compliments on the decor or his cooking (though he often received them). His hospitality was not a performance. His goal was not praise. His expectation from such get-togethers was not selfish. His hope was simply to share life with others and bring gladness.

Gary did not believe hospitality was optional in Christian life. Scripture, after all, enjoins believers to "practice hospitality,"[3] to welcome the stranger, and to be generous with one's bounty. Gary was struck—he told me so—at how often Jesus is pictured at meal settings in the Bible, and Gary was convinced that, whether they want to or not, the followers of Christ are expected to open their homes and share their tables. For Gary, though, it was not mere duty. He was certain that hospitality— like prayer, worship, community, and Scripture— was given to us as a source of joy and as a means of drawing close to God and one another.

Gary believed that there was something deeply holy—and deeply pleasant—about gathering for a meal. My guess is that anyone leaving his house did so with the feeling that they had been genuinely welcome and that Gary had really wanted them to be there.

Because he did.

I DON'T KNOW THAT he was ever aware of the Benedictine Rule, but Gary practiced it admirably and often: "All guests who present themselves are to be welcomed as Christ."

There was something that Gary did quite commonly at the conclusion of meals. He would choose a book—often Spurgeon's *Morning and Evening*, Baillie's *Diary of Private Prayer*, or Scripture—and read a page, a paragraph, a line. Then he would ask for permission to say a prayer. No one, to my knowledge, ever refused him.

One by one, he would pray for each individual at the table, expressing thanks for them, commending their strengths, and asking help for their weaknesses or needs. He used words that were common, conversational, and practical. Rarely did I hear Gary on those occasions, on any occasion really, that tears didn't become part of his prayer, as if to emphasize that words could never be adequate nor eloquent enough for what he wanted to express.

For some, it might have been a bit awkward, weird even, but I never got the sense that people were ungrateful.

And then, at the end of those evenings, it became Gary's routine, especially after he took up woodworking as a hobby, to give each person a gift as they were leaving his house.

I FELT AN UNEASINESS as I went through Gary's personal belongings after he passed away. Places I would never have dreamed of trespassing—desk drawers, closed boxes, file cabinets, envelopes—now *required* my attention. There were times that the process made me ill. I wanted Gary's permission to be there or, better yet, his explanation as to what I was looking at on many occasions. I could only bear those reminders of his absence for a short while at a time. Being around them was like holding my breath underwater. I quickly found myself needing more air than the rooms contained.

His woodworking shop made me feel much the same, different only in that the items there—wood, boards, hand tools—seemed more alive, more like Gary somehow, than paperwork and file boxes.

I found a small leather-bound journal on one of the work-tables in the shop. It measures four inches by six inches and has a shoestring-length leather strip that can be wrapped and tied to hold it closed. The pages are unruled. Gary used it to keep a record of wood pieces that he made and gave away. The opening caption says: "Woodturning, Begun May/June 2007." Below that, and on following pages, are five columns: date, item, wood, given to, and number. An entry might read, and one in fact does: "July 24, 2007, bowl, spalted maple, Berta Alston, 33."

From May 7, 2007, through August 19, 2008, Gary made 248 entries in that book, which means that scattered around the world are 248 bowls, goblets, boxes, vases, pens, and candle-sticks that passed through his hands as tokens of affection.

I'm not sure why Gary felt compelled to keep that list—maybe just to remember, maybe to keep up with inventory, maybe to chronicle his progress as a woodturner, maybe to ensure that all the people most special to him had received something—but I do know that he did *not* keep it as a record of his generosity or goodness. He never meant, nor expected, for anyone to read those entries but himself.

The logbook also contains an entry that Gary "took trip to wood-turning school in Utah" from July 8–13, 2007.

Two other entries record that work was put on hold while he went to Afghanistan for three and a half months in late 2007 and for two months in the autumn of 2008.

Another shows him gone to Spain and Holland from April 16–27, 2008.

Conspicuously absent from the logbook is any column for money matters—expenses, receivables, income, profit, loss—the kinds of things that good business people usually record in ledgers. Truth is, Gary took great delight in giving, in sharing, in using his material possessions—his "stuff"—to enrich others.

Another woodworker had been his inspiration.

Gary did eventually sell a few, very few, of the things he produced in his shop—it was, after all, his full-time vocation when he was home—but he gave away the vast majority of pieces, often to his dinner guests as part of the farewell ritual.

Even now, people will often tell me of the time that Gary gave them a gift from his shop. I've been in a number of homes where, first thing, someone wants to show me an item that was made specifically for them.

And they are right in asserting that the gift was *for them*. Gary once told me that whenever he worked on a new piece, he always had in mind the person to whom it would be given.

As he worked, he would pray for that person. It might well be that the best and most enduring gift that Gary delivered was not the visible, tangible object, but the prayers it represented. Those cups and bowls and boxes, empty to the eyes, were full of invisible treasure, the incense of prayer.

I don't know why the logbook entries ended in August 2008. I do know that he continued to give away most of what he made.

JUST A FEW WEEKS before Gary's diagnosis, he had rented a booth at a local galleria—little more than a glorified flea market—in hopes that it might be a place to sell some of his woodwork. He set up a beautiful display of bowls, small tables, miscellaneous collectibles, and his greatest novelty—wooden cowboy hats. (Our early question when Gary showed us the first such creation was, "How does he make those things?" It was soon replaced with "*Why?*") His exhibit, if I can say so without seeming to brag, was notably more thought-out and tasteful than those of his neighbors, most of whom seemed intent on merely cleaning out their tool rooms and attics. The prices of Gary's merchandise were substantially higher than the dimes and dollars being asked by other vendors for their used paperbacks and secondhand kitchenware. Gary's booth garnered lots of traffic and generated considerable praise but not much in the way of sales.

When we learned of Gary's cancer, the items in his booth suddenly took on a new importance to me and the rest of the family. They immediately became rarities. (The doctor told us that Gary's failing eyesight would make it dangerous and inadvisable for him to work with sawblades any longer.) If he was at the end of his woodworking days, and if he had previously given most of his pieces away, then it meant no new items would be forthcoming. There would be no more "Gary originals." Those in our possession quickly became priceless to us.

Gary thought otherwise.

In one of his many lighthearted moments—or maybe he was being serious—he suggested that we have a "Dying of Cancer Sale."

"I guarantee you we can double the price," he said. "And we'll sell every one of them."

We laughed—and promptly vetoed the idea.

We closed the booth and brought the items home.

IN THE BIBLE, THERE is the story of a woman named Dorcas. She is remembered as one "who was always doing good and helping the poor." Scripture records that after she died, her friends wept and showed the Apostle Peter "the robes and other clothing that Dorcas had made while she was still with them."⁴ They were handmade mementoes of her life, things that were personal, beautiful, and useful.

Gary left such things behind. Most special to me is a round dining room table that he made out of heart pine. We were in my vegetable garden one day, during the time he was making the table, when I noticed him looking with particular interest at one of the fence posts surrounding the garden, a stout four-by-four corner post that I had painted white. He asked me if he could remove it and put another in its place. It turns out Gary needed one more piece of wood for a table leg, a piece that would match the other three, and the corner post in my garden, unbeknownst to me, was heart pine.

On the bottom of the table, woodburned in Gary's inimitable script, are the words, "To Allen, my best friend and brother. I love you, Gary. 4-19-2010. Perhaps today."

The table, to me, is a fit and beautiful tribute to Gary's practice of hospitality. It encourages me to follow his example—shared meals, slow food, good conversation, quiet house.

It also brings to mind a conversation we had during his illness. I asked him what he wanted me to do with his house after he was gone. He simply said, "Use it to bless people. You'll know what to do."

I ANTICIPATED THAT AFTER Gary died it would be emotionally difficult to enter his house for the first time. Even while he was sick, when I had to retrieve something from there, I found myself ill at ease as I realized that those walls, within which so much goodness had been acted out, would know his presence no longer. Already the place had a sense of enormous emptiness and was only a shell of its better self. The house, in a way, had become a dying body too.

A couple of days after Gary's funeral and after most of the family had returned to their homes, we—Dad, Mom, Beth, and I—went to Gary's house together. When we opened the door and walked in, I think it hit us all the same way—poignant with memory, but air too thin to breathe.

Another Afghanistan.

The emotional reaction to entering the house was predictable, struck as we all were with the sense of what once was and would never be again. That table. Those chairs. The good ghosts of all those who had gathered and shared that space through the years.

It might have been on the first occasion of going into Gary's house, or it might have been later, but I remember clearly a time when the implements in his kitchen, the pots and pans in particular, caught my attention. They had taken on the personality of their owner; they were commonplace, used up, inelegant. Had I not known better, I could easily have mistaken them for the tools of some old miner, used to sift through stream water and silt to pan for gold. The surfaces, inside and out, were scarred, scorched, scratched, worn thin, very tired.

Perhaps miner he was.

With those long-handled, deep-bottomed, oddly-shaped bits of copper, cast-iron, and aluminum, Gary had brought forth treasures of conversation and neighborliness. They unearthed the hearts of many—rough mixtures of gold and mud—to be washed in prayer and refined for goodness. They were utensils of grace.

I've a hunch that in all the places Gary lived, he had pots and pans just like those he used at home. All of those dishes really do belong in a shrine somewhere.

SOMETIMES I GO TO Gary's house and sit for a while. At present, it is almost bare. The table and chairs are still where they always were. The chair in which he used to sit each morning to read and pray is still there. Other than that, it's empty. I can close my eyes and remember Young Life gatherings that took place in that room. I can remember house concerts I played there. I can hear the laughter of Mac Turner, John Gay, and Bobby Joe Baxley. I can picture Gary and Bill Goans rocking on the front porch, telling stories. I can recall countless times that Gary and I shared a simple lunch together at that table of oak.

Good ghosts.

When Gary used to say a blessing before the meal, he almost always concluded with words like these: "Lord, we invite You to be our Honored Guest. Please enjoy this meal with us."

And I think the Lord did just that.

Wherever Gary lived, he was neighborly, in the most literal sense of the word. I saw it when I was with him for a few days in Afghanistan. He knew the people (the men anyway) on his street. They knew him.

When he was introducing me to Mazar-e-Sharif in the summer of 2006, he didn't take me on a tour of buildings. Instead, he took me to people. We went to the rug shop to meet Reza, the shop owner. He took me to a roadside kiosk to meet Daveed. He introduced me to Fawad and Najibullah, who could serve as interpreters for me. He asked them to take good care of me, a request that is taken seriously by Pashtun men. He helped me interview and choose the fifteen young men who would be in my conversational English class. He took me for walks around the city with his former students. And wherever he went, he knew people by name. He greeted them, and they responded, warmly.

Dad saw the same friendliness at work in Macedonia. The folks in the street greeted Gary—calling him "Levi," the name he chose for himself when he was abroad—and the sight of him cheered them.

Wherever he lived, he took pains to know and befriend the people closest to him.

His reasoning was simple: "You can't love your neighbors if you don't know them."

When Gary lived in Spain, he moved into a sizable apartment complex. His first few days there he went to every unit in the building and introduced himself to its residents. He took small gifts to each of them, flowers or sweets or a bottle of wine. His Spanish was broken at best, and I have no idea how he began those introductions. My guess is that a number of them were spoken to faces half-hidden through barely-opened doors—but probably only half-hidden for a minute or so.

I can tell you what Gary's neighbors saw if they *did* open their doors: They saw a kind face; they saw eyes that were glad to see them, that fixed intently on them when they spoke. They received a handshake, two-handed, and very likely a soft pat on the shoulder. I would be very surprised if he did not invite them to please, please, call him if he could ever help them in any way. He would tell them that he was grateful and happy to be their neighbor. And he would mean it. He would try to learn all of their names.

Soon he would know the neighborhood restaurants and pubs. He would know where he could go to watch soccer with the locals, where he might have a meal or buy someone a beer.

Within days of going to a new country to live, Gary would always send us a letter (or, in time, an email) with a list of names of people to pray for—the names of coworkers, the names of students, the names of neighbors.

And at each place, his kitchen, like the one in Hamilton, would become a gathering place where those names might come together to talk and to share life.

I was talking to a young man recently who said he wants to live life in such a way that people can see, through him, what God is like. It's a lofty aspiration, but consistent with the admonition that we be "imitators of God . . . and live a life of love."[5]

A dinner table is a good place to put the gifts of God on display: the living word (conversation), the bread of life (a well-prepared meal), the rose of Sharon (a touch of beauty), the open door (a welcome), and the pearl of great price (a gift upon departing).

At Gary's table, many saw what God is like.

I THOUGHT I WAS done writing this chapter and had said all I needed to say, when I got an email from Afghanistan. I have received others like it since Gary's passing, but this one seemed to arrive by appointment, to impress upon me that all the things I'm sharing with you about Gary are not merely the affectionate exaggerations of a sentimental brother but indeed an accurate record of an actual life. Here is how a man on the other side of the world, with somewhat broken English, remembers Gary's life and describes his hospitable kindness:

> From: Noor M. R_____
> Date: May 31, 2015 at 3:50:02 AM CDT
> Subj: NOOR: A student of Gary Levi from Afghanistan
>
> Dear Sir/Madam,
>
> Gary Levi taught me English and he spent hours of his life sitting in a classroom to let me know something in 2007. He spoke to me a lot about Jesus! He accepted my invitation and came to my home to have dinner and he offered me to go to his house, have some food, and chat for long times. I really loved the way he spoke about his believes and offering to come to help Afghanistan people. The last time I saw him was sometime in mid 2009 and he showed me the last page of his Bible that my name was among many other names listed, he told me "Noor, I pray for you every morning! Make sure you pray for me!" then we said goodbye.
>
> It has been a long time that I have this puzzle in my mind that why my dearest teacher is not answering

my Email. Finally I went to check my notebook from 2009 today to see some notes of teacher Levi. He gave the address (www.allenlevi.com) one day and told me: "Noor if I didn't answer your Emails for a very long time then check this website". Today was the day to check the website! Now I know everything! I have lost my teacher and I can't believe this! All my prayers for my dearest teacher and his family! I am sure he some where in heaven listening to Jesus!

Teacher Gary helped a poor boy to learn English and today that poor boy is having a job and supporting a family!

God bless you and your family my teacher!

Your student Noor

Beth and I answered Noor's email separately and received this reply:

Dear Ms. Leikvold and Mr. Levi,

Teacher G. Levi was a gift to the very lucky ones and I am extremely happy that I am one of those lucky people. When I first met teacher Gary, I was 20 years old and in that age beside being my teacher he accepted to be my friend. He was a very good listener. One day he listened to me for more than 3 hours. All I was telling him was about rough time that I had when Taliban attacked my village and killed thousands of our people. Sometime the real help is to listen to someone and teacher Gary really helped me. Sometime I cried and he gave me examples of Jesus and cured my wounds! Sometime he played guitar to me and we sang songs together "This is the day that the lord has made." Sometimes he said jokes and made me laugh! Sometime he did magic tricks and made me feel amazed! I remember every single second I spent with teacher Gary and I will remember his quotes and lessons to the end of my life.

In advance I would love to thank you all for your nice prayers you did for me and my family. The reason I am living in this critical situation of my country is your prayers. In my job, I do travel a lot to many unsecured areas and I am still safe and nothing happens to me! God may keep you safe and bless you all!

Noor, a student of teacher Gary Levi

Terms

BEFORE I GO FURTHER, it might be helpful to add a note of explanation for the sake of clarity.

I try not to use religious jargon, laden as it is with so much misunderstanding and negative connotation. Such terms— repentance, atonement, reconciliation, judgment, right, wrong, even love, forgiveness—can be objectionable and obsolete to modern minds. Many of these terms used to bother me too. I can remember times when they have felt (and still feel) like weapons and walls, misused or manipulated to exclude and imply moral superiority.

I have learned, however, to treasure the realities that these words stand for, the truth behind them, and the hope they represent when taken together. I choose to use some of them because they were ones that Gary used and because they are still the best words for the story they tell.

I hope you'll not mind if I give simple definitions to several of them since I'll be using them from time to time.

Jesus Christ: the flawless man, born to Mary in Bethlehem, who embodied perfect love and is uniquely *the* Son of God; the one through whom humankind is forgiven of its sins and misdeeds, bought out of its various slaveries, adopted into the family of God, and empowered to live lives of love. He is sometimes referred to as Lord, King, Emmanuel ("God with us"), or Savior.

Gospel: the message concerning Jesus Christ and the Kingdom of God; the nonfiction story through which humankind is rescued from its brokenness and returned to intimacy with God.

Christian: a person who professes belief in the teachings of Jesus Christ, who trusts in the death and resurrection of Christ for his or her rescue from the power and penalty of sin, who loves and lives in submission to Jesus Christ.

Sin: anything less than perfect love—perfect love for God, for our neighbors, for ourselves. Everything wrong with the world, ever, is the result of sin.

Missionary: in the Christian context, one who serves Jesus Christ by taking the gospel to all the world. This term should not be confused with "humanitarian," a person who does good works to help people—a noble thing—but without particular concern for sharing the story of Christ. In some sense, all Christians are missionaries, enjoined to live and to tell the Gospel. Some, like Gary, do that work vocationally, full-time.

Each of these small words, and all the others that I won't belabor you with, are substantial in their scope and implications, somewhat like the simple formula $e=mc^2$. It takes seconds to write them down or say them, but a lot of work to ever understand them. These definitions might help you better understand and grasp the contours of Gary's heart. That's not to say you will agree with him. But it might make clear that he had a definite aim in life—to share a message that deals with the direst need and meets the deepest longings of the human soul.

Gathering

WHILE GARY FREQUENTLY HAD small gatherings at his house, there were other, more infrequent, occasions where his fondness for celebration became the stuff of family legend.

When Mom and Dad reached fifty years of marriage, Gary masterminded a week's worth of events to commemorate that milestone. The first of those events was on a Sunday afternoon, September 22, 2002.

The plan was this: Gary invited Dad and Mom to supper, something he did often. (This was before they had moved to the farm to live. They were still in a house in Columbus at the time.) He came up with some ruse for why he and I would pick them up in the middle of the afternoon. He told them to dress nicely since he was going to take them somewhere special—that too was not out of the ordinary for him.

Gary, the benevolent conniver, had called a family friend, one of considerable wealth, to ask if we might borrow his Learjet that night. "And while I'm asking, could we borrow your pilot too?"

I'm certain that, being the gentleman he was, Gary offered to cover all expenses for the usage. Except that when the friend found out what Gary was planning, he wanted to be part of the celebration himself by lending the jet, picking up the tab, and making sure that champagne and roses were on the plane when we stepped aboard. Gary gladly allowed him to do so.

Beth, Linda, and Laura were waiting beside the plane at the local airport when Gary and I drove up with Mom and Dad. There was plenty of grandstanding and disbelieving laughter as the excursion began.

When Mom and Dad had married on September 27, 1952, it had been in a very small, family-only ceremony—all they could afford at the time—at the home of Mom's parents in a community called Pisgah, near Summit, Mississippi.

They had honeymooned in New Orleans.

So . . .

Gary had arranged for us to fly to New Orleans that night. We arrived in late afternoon, caught a white stretch limo into the city, had coffee somewhere quiet so we could ask Dad and Mom to tell us stories of their courtship and marriage, ate supper at a swanky restaurant, and then flew home that same evening. We left New Orleans late, just ahead of a big Louisiana storm.

Gary—the most un-Learjet, unfancy person you might ever meet—had pulled off an afternoon and evening of unforgettable fancy.

For the following week, there were events every day—a breakfast for the extended family, planned visits with old friends, giving of gifts (including a new car to Mom), and finally a big barbecue and chapel service at the farm where Dad and Mom renewed their wedding vows.

Gary beamed whenever he could turn a spotlight or, as we say at the Longstreet Church, "pin a rose" on someone he loved. Those almost-perfect days he attempted to orchestrate were, to him, a chance to share something heavenly—"a fore-taste of glory divine"—with his friends. I'm not quite sure I know the word that best describes the feeling of those gatherings—gladness, merriment, exuberance, holiness?—but Gary wanted us to partake of it whether we knew what it was called or not. He derived great joy from the thought that some such gathering, one that he'd convened, might be a window through which others would get a glimpse into the Kingdom of God.

For sure, he wanted the sheer sweetness of the occasion—the existential fullness of being at that very place at that precise moment with those exact people—to bless all in attendance, but he believed that such moments always pointed to something bigger, and he hoped, I am certain, that those present might trace the whatever-it-was they were feeling all the way to the Source.

"Taste and see," he might have added to the invitations. "Come to this gathering, where we'll eat and tell stories and sit outside without clocks, and where we will laugh and learn about one another, where we'll taste and see that the Lord is good."

ON A CLEAR, UNUSUALLY mild morning in February 1998, a Saturday, I was sitting on the porch of the big house with Dad, Mom, and Gary. An unfamiliar vehicle, a van, approached the house. Turns out that one of my former college roommates, whom I'd not seen in years—he was a pharmacist who lived with his wife and children near Orlando—had come by for an unannounced visit.

"Just happened to be in the neighborhood and thought we'd stop by."

He had several of his children with him. I was more than a little surprised and more than a little delighted to see them all. Lamar Edwards—Laroo, we called him—was one of the most gloriously, winsomely big souls that I've ever met. Still is.

We had barely begun catching up on all the years that had passed since we'd last seen each other, and I was still confounded by the unlikeliness of such a visit, when another vehicle, also unexpected, pulled up the driveway. It was Ben and Sally May, dear friends from Birmingham.

"Just happened to be in the neighborhood."

Within minutes, another vehicle and then another, all on unannounced visits, made their way up the dirt road to the house, vehicles bearing license plates from across the Southeast and carrying childhood friends, college classmates, law partners, and family.

It was all Gary's doing.

I had forgotten that it was February 5th.

Gary, as he always did, remembered.

I was born on May 24, 1956. But February 5, 1978, was the day, at least the day I am conscious of, when I began my walk with Christ. It was the day, to use Jesus' term, that I was "born again," reborn, made new, "saved." Gary had calculated that on February 5, 1998, my life had been neatly divided in half. For my first twenty-one years, I had lived largely oblivious to and altogether unsurrendered to Christ; and now, for the past twenty-one years, I had lived attentive and increasingly surrendered to Him.

On that day, my lost years equaled my found ones.

To Gary, that was arithmetic worth celebrating. To him, this was the birthday that mattered most of all. There would be yet another, a third one, at which angels would be in attendance. But for now, Gary wanted to throw a party in honor of a rebirth.

For months, from his home overseas, he had planned the party with the help of friends and family. They kept their conspiracy of kindness a secret. I can only guess how much deception was employed to keep me in the dark and to assure my presence at home that weekend. And while I was a bit embarrassed at the trouble they had gone to on my behalf, I had a distinct sense that their joy at bringing so memorable an occasion together was as deep as my own that day.

Many of the people who showed up had known each other in years past but had not seen each other for a long time. Gary was master of ceremonies to what felt like a class reunion, wedding, dinner on the grounds, tent revival, and pregame Saturday tailgating all rolled into one.

And it was all to celebrate that "I once was lost / but now am found / was blind but now I see." The event was *for* me, but it was not *about* me.

After the meal, the gathering moved from the barn to the chapel at the edge of the pasture. Gary had asked several of the guests to make some comments, or, to use a phrase that I've heard in African American churches, to "speak over" me. (That phrase is usually reserved for funerals, as in, "At this point in our service, we will ask brother Hudson to come speak over Deacon Floyd." "Eulogize" might be an equivalent term.)

In truth, the experience was a bit Tom Sawyer-esque. I was attending my own funeral, where the rules of veracity were all suspended in the name of charity, and the speakers were obligated to say only nice things about me.

For a couple of hours, we sat together and shared the hair-trigger laughter of people who had history together and were comfortable in each other's presence. There were happy tears of gratitude, and everyone seemed conscious of the gift it was to be with those people in that place at that moment.

Gary's intent had been to honor and encourage me that day, and he succeeded. But be assured: While not meant to be so, it was much more a celebration and display of *his* life than mine. Those who "just happened to be in the neighborhood" that morning could not help but be moved by the thoughtfulness and unselfishness—Gary's—that had brought us all together. All of the kind things said about me were nothing but the deflected praise that was due him. And I think everyone there was conscious of that fact— everyone except Gary.

If you could have read his mind that day, this is what I think you would have found in Gary's thoughts: "This, in a tiny way, is what heaven is like. This is how it looks when we love the right things in the right way. This is what it means to walk with God. It is so very good."

The buttons all lined up that day.

It was a Saturday for the ages.

Song

IT WAS A PRONOUNCED and sometimes humorous trait of Gary's to seek out and learn new things. Such pursuits were always wholehearted even if they were short-lived.

For example:

During his high school years—I believe it was after he began running the mile on the track team—Gary got it into his head that he could be a javelin thrower. I think his logic went something like this: a) not many people do it, so competition will be slight and chance of success high; b) training in javelin cannot be nearly as grueling as that required to compete in the mile; and c) I am physically strong and naturally wiry, attributes well-suited to the sport. He may have gotten additional inspiration from watching the summer Olympic games that year on television.

My recollection of the details is sketchy—exactly what he threw (I know he never owned a javelin), how he developed his technique (I know he never got any coaching for the sport), or what encouragement he was given by third parties (I know he got little to none from his family). What I do know is that for a period of time in the early 1970s, the backyard of 2404 Carson Drive was one of the most dangerous patches of real estate in any non-combat zone on the planet. Gary threw his spear from one end of the yard to the other. East to west. West to east. Death by javelin—"drive-by spearing"—was a considerable threat until Gary's javelin fever was dethroned by a sudden and intense interest in training bird dogs.

Stay with me. There is a point to my telling you this.

After Gary graduated from UGA with a degree in Agricultural Economics, he took employment with Dad in the timber business. Dad, by that time, owned a sawmill in Shiloh—Pineco Inc.—and needed a certified lumber grader, someone who could look at lumber and determine its quality for sale. The higher the quality of a board (fewer knots, straighter grain, absence of blemishes, etc.), the higher its value.

Gary was tapped to be the Pineco lumber grader. To obtain the required training and education, he went to Haywood Community College in Clyde, North Carolina. He was there for a year or so.

When Gary got to Appalachia, he found himself in a world of mountain people for whom banjo, fiddle, and guitar were parts of the native tongue. Having long been a fan of bluegrass music, he took up banjo with all the enthusiasm of a javelin thrower.

But this time, the passion lasted.

Prior to banjo, Gary had played guitar, quite nicely I might add, and knew something of fingerpicking patterns. (He was timid about playing guitar in front of people, but I did get him to accompany me in Greg and Beth's wedding ceremony at the farm chapel in January 1981.) Banjo, therefore, was not a dive into the totally unfamiliar. He began practicing, watched others closely, and in time became an excellent player. He bought a high-end banjo and, when he returned to Georgia, practiced and played consistently. I've a hunch that if he'd had a band of other bluegrass players to work with on a regular basis, he'd have become a player of some renown. He had steady rhythm, a nice sense of melody, a sweet voice that held pitch, the discipline to explore and improve, and a deep belief in the power of music to do good.

When Gary went overseas, his banjo often went with him.

Now fly to the other end of the musical spectrum—cool jazz.

I don't recall when or why he suddenly took an interest in the saxophone. He might have been inspired by the songs of Kenny G, an immensely popular player in the '80s and '90s. Whatever the inspiration, Gary decided to play the horn.

And so, with the same intensity that he had brought to track, javelin, bird dogs, deer hunting, chess, cycling, sleight of hand, tree husbandry, stock trading, and other passing interests, Gary undertook saxophonery.

He ordered instructional materials, recordings, and a good instrument. Before long, he was an impressive and—dare I say it of my Southern-to-the-bone, bluegrassy, bird-doggish brother—soulful horn player.

HERE IS A MEMORY I treasure: When Gary was in the States, he would sometimes sit on his porch in the evening, weather permitting, and play the horn. He had learned a number of hymns and had stylized them with his own bends and trills so that they almost seemed vocal in the glorious tradition of black gospel songs. The pond between my house and his served as a resonator, and the sound—already warm and airy, true to the personality of the sax—would roll across the pasture, pick up some bird song, and land on my porch.

The horn, like the banjo, became another of Gary's traveling companions. I don't know the extent to which he performed overseas, but I recall pictures of him standing streetside in Eastern Europe, playing his saxophone to gather a crowd.

I have often been asked if Gary could sing well. "Beauti-fully so," is always my answer, even if he was shy about doing it in public.

He loved to sing. I recall a snow skiing trip we took to Colorado one winter. For many years, we made an annual trip out west, and even to Europe a couple of times, to fine-tune our very own, very unpolished brand of downhill skiing.

That particular Colorado trip might have been the one when Gary, no fan of fashion, skied for days in an oversized pair of fluorescent orange coveralls. He was a size L; they were XXLs. ("But I got 'em at a great price!") At any distance and among any crowd, he was as easy to spot as a ball of flame coming down the mountain.

It was Gary's suggestion that, while there, we memorize some hymns together. By then we could ski well enough, or daringly enough, to go to the tops of the mountains, which meant that we had considerable time to practice the songs on the longer ski lifts. And Gary thought it would be good to practice them at considerable volume.

I don't recall all the songs we learned, but I do have clear memory of "Joyful, Joyful, We Adore Thee," a song apropos to the mountain grandeur of the Rockies. We would sing all the verses en route to the black diamonds. I can only imagine what the people who rode the lift chairs in front of and behind us might have thought—some, I am certain, were more glad than usual to reach the top of the mountain and get off of the lift.

No one ever complimented us on our singing, but I think Gary harbored the hope that someone might have heard something helpful in the sublime lyrics of the songs we sang.

All that said, it is no surprise that music was very much a part of Gary's last year.

On July 29, 2011, a Friday, six days after we learned of Gary's cancer, he was scheduled for a diagnostic procedure called needle biopsy. By then, it had already been ascertained by the doctors, based on brain scans, that the tumor was not safely operable. The needle biopsy was scheduled to determine more precisely the nature of Gary's illness so that treatment options could be explored. It required insertion of a small probe through the skull and collection of a tiny piece of the tumor. The procedure was not too complicated as surgeries go and didn't take very long to perform, but it did require that Gary stay overnight in the intensive care unit (ICU). That evening while he rested, I placed an iPad on his pillow, the volume turned down very low, in hopes that music might drown out the hums, buzzes, clicks, and other noises of hardware and misery that were constant reminders of where he was. I sat with Gary in his room until the nurse made me leave for the night.

Before I left, he asked if he could sing a song for me. He'd never done that before. What followed was an extemporaneous composition, a prayer, in which he used my name often and asked God to care for me. In that same song, he called the name of a niece who was going through a difficult season in her life.

I left the ICU to spend the night in the visitors' waiting lounge, eager to rejoin Gary as soon as they opened the doors the next morning.

There were no separate rooms in the ICU, only thin curtains dividing the patients from one another. It was very easy to hear sounds up and down the hallway.

During the night, the battery to the iPad either gave out or Gary forgot how to keep it running. It went silent.

Early the following morning, as soon as visitors were admitted to the unit, I heard Gary singing as I approached. Before pulling back the curtain, I stopped to listen. I'd never heard the song before and realized after a few seconds that he was again making one up, impromptu. He was singing to God. There was a lot of repetition, sometimes just phrases with frequent invocations of Jesus' name. The melody was simple, easy to repeat, hymnic. I stood outside the curtain for a little while and let Gary sing.

When I finally walked in, he told me that at the far end of the ICU from where he was situated, another patient, a man, had moaned ceaselessly throughout the night. I had heard that noise when I left the ICU eight hours earlier. And it *was* loud, bothersome, and inescapable, a vocal reminder that we were in a place for very sick, very hurt people.

During the night, Gary had begun singing out of exasperation (he was a light sleeper), hoping to drown out the noises of the moaning man.

When one of the nurses made her rounds that night, Gary asked her what was wrong with the fellow. Gary had assumed that the moans were hallucinatory or psychological or drug-induced. He learned from the nurse that the man was in severe pain. The groans were pure, raw hurt. The revelation troubled Gary deeply. He cried when he told me about it. His reflex had been to help the man, to reach out to the far end of the hall and offer some kind of comfort, but bedbound and immobile himself, there was only one thing he could do: He sang.

He knew it would take considerable volume to reach the man, but sing Gary did, loudly and persistently.

Ski-lift loud.

Gary told me he had tried to choose words that might bring hope to the poor man. Whether they actually reached his ears, his mind, or his soul, I can't say. We never knew who he was or what became of him, but I think Gary harbored the hope, as he had toward others on the mountains of Colorado and in the streets of Eastern Europe, that the sound of music might communicate something healing and good to the moaning man.

For weeks afterward, Gary often chuckled as he imagined what the nurses, techs, and other patients must have thought as they listened to and endured the competing voices of that night. Dueling banjos. Call and response.

Cries of hurt.

Songs of hope.

> Melt the clouds of sin and sadness,
> Drive the dark of doubt away,
> Giver of immortal gladness,
> Fill us with the light of day.
>
> . . .
>
> Joyful, joyful, we adore Thee,
> God of glory, Lord of love.[6]

THOUGH I HAD DECIDED to curtail all of my work until Gary's sickness resolved itself one way or another, I did try to remain musical during that time. Gary encouraged me to do so. Early on, when Beth and I were working out the logistics of the cancer season and my desire to be home with Gary, we came to a quick decision that we would accept no further bookings and, if possible, would cancel everything already on the calendar. Thankfully, the groups who had already booked me were gracious and understanding. Almost everything came off the schedule, and for the first time in fifteen years, my calendar was entirely clear.

There was one cancellation that posed a bit of a challenge. Just three weeks after Gary's diagnosis, I was scheduled to play at a prestigious gathering to benefit the Springer Opera House in Columbus. In 1971 the venue had been designated the State Theatre of Georgia by then-Governor Jimmy Carter. The fundraiser was a black-tie event. The present governor of Georgia would be in attendance, and I would be singing on at least one number with the governor's daughter, Katie. Invitations had been sent out, and I had begun writing and preparing for the event long before Gary got sick.

My intention was to cancel, even over Gary's strong insistence that I play the event. I made an appointment with Paul Pierce, a quick-witted, kindhearted soul who served as artistic director of the Springer. Paul had hired me for the event. By the time we met at his office, just days after Gary's diagnosis, he had already heard the news. He expressed his concern for me and the family. I stated the obvious to him—that I was in a place of extreme distraction, that I was damaged goods, that I didn't want to ruin their event, and that I had come to cancel. He didn't flinch, but said something along the lines of: "We still want you. If you can't rehearse with your musicians, that's okay. If you can't write anything new, that's okay. If you come with just your guitar and play a song or two, that would be fine."

I was hoping he would all too gladly release me from my commitment and find a suitable replacement. Instead, I left the meeting having promised I'd be at the gala and would do the best I could.

A musical friend of mine once coined a lyrical phrase—"the choreography of coinci-dance"—to describe the way that God orchestrates circumstances in our lives for good purpose. At any given moment, especially when suffering is involved, it can be difficult to discern anything positive. But from a distance, we sometimes gain clarity.

In my years as a performing musician, I have lived with a conviction that the concerts I've played were scheduled, chosen, ordained by God for good purpose, even if on bad nights I could not possibly have told myself what that purpose might be.

As I approached the night of the Springer event, I had a sense that the "choreography of coinci-dance" was at work, and that the gala converged with the revelation of Gary's cancer for a reason. Perhaps, I thought, I was supposed to bring *my* story to the stage that night. After all, most of the people in the audience were from the community where Gary and I had spent most of our lives; they were friends and acquaintances. Most of them would already be aware of Gary's condition, many loved him and our family, and they would know what was most deeply on my mind that night.

A day or two before the gala, I began to write a story about two brothers, about a king and a princess, about fear and reluctance. And then I wrote a song. I didn't do so, at least not at the outset, with any thought of sharing either of them publicly. I merely wrote the pieces, as I have countless others through the years, to help me process what I was going through at the time.

As I continued to write, however, it began to stir in me that maybe, somehow, I was *supposed* to share them at the Springer. I didn't want to inflict my grief on the audience, or bring my heaviness to a festive occasion, but I felt little by little that the song and story were meant to be part of the evening. And so, at dress rehearsal, when I was working with the other musicians, I played the song for them and asked for their counsel on whether to end the concert with it or not. I knew them well and trusted their judgment more than my own. They said yes.

I approached the evening of the gala with a keen sense that I was there to sing for Gary. I had arranged for him, Mom, and Dad to come as my guests and to sit in the balcony, front and center, since it would be empty. He had always been my most ardent encourager, along with Beth, and it was heavily in my mind that this might be the last time he would hear me play on stage.

I was not oblivious to the others in the room; it would have been unkind, selfish, arrogant, and dishonest to be so. But in my mind, Gary was the guest of honor that night.

Of all the performances in my musical life, this is the one I will never forget.

I could not see Gary because of the spotlights, but I knew exactly where he was sitting. At the end of the night, for my last selection, I shared the story of the two brothers.

There are rare times in a songwriter's work, at least there have been for me, when something transcendent takes place in the performance of a song, when all the hearts in the room are fully present but, at the same time, fully taken away—to the true, the good, the holy. The feeling at such moments is not "me" the performer and "them" the audience, but "us" together, us under the gaze and in the grip of God.

For me, my brother and I were the only people in the room at that moment; but, somehow, there was all the richness of a worshipping congregation. A life—Gary's—focused our thoughts, a story of love drew us in, a song of hope opened our hearts.

That was indeed the last time that Gary ever saw me play publicly. But actually, it was not *my* performance. It was *ours*, Gary's and mine. It took a lifetime together to write that song and that story. It took fifty-four years to set the stage for that night, for that moment when two hearts, held together by and overflowing with friendship and affection, broke open unreservedly.

> *Set the stage, tune the fiddle,*
> *Call the dancers, call the clowns,*
> *Dress the children in the colors of the spring,*
> *When life hits you with a riddle,*
> *And the answer can't be found,*
> *All join hands, and do this simple thing:*
>
> *Sing a song, tell a story,*
> *Be reminded of what matters most of all,*

Sing a song, tell a story,
Be reminded of what matters most of all.

Get your closest friends together,
Tell some tales of days gone by,
Talk of travels, talk of troubles, talk of dreams,
In the face of angry weather,
When you simply want to cry,
Gather round, and let the music ring.

No matter how bleak the hour,
No matter how deep the sting,
No matter how steep the mountain,
Sing, brother, sing.

Sing the song, tell the Story,
To remind us of what matters most of all.
Sing the song, tell the Story,
To remind us of what matters most of all.[7]

Yet and still, brother the younger says: "Sing."

MANY YEARS AGO, I wrote a lyric about how much I enjoy playing music "for one or less." The thought still holds true.

The cancer season gave me ample opportunity to act on that preference. There were frequent occasions when I played my guitar for Gary while he rested or slept. Some of those "noodlings" turned into songs, but most of them, made up on the spot, had a life span of one performance.

I am a mediocre guitar player at best, but Gary was generous with his compliments and thanks, and playing at his bedside—seeing his countenance calm and his body rest—was as gratifying as anything I've ever done musically. His affirmation—"Bah, that's beautiful. Who wrote that?"—was praise of the highest order.

Have you ever wondered why we have music? Life would carry on just fine without it. Less pleasantly perhaps, but fine. If you had asked Gary, he would have told you that pleasure, in whatever form it takes—the taste of chocolate, the presence of color, the telling of stories—is a signpost to God.

To Gary, heaven was present with a thousand daily voices in this world, which explains to me why he found life so endlessly interesting. In the grain of a cherry burl, the intricacy of a feather, the aroma of cooking meat, the adrenalin rush of jumping off a mountain to ride a thermal, the unfathomable span of a night sky, the timbre of woodwinds, the mating call of turkeys, the restlessness of a soul in search of God—in all of these Gary found reason for contemplation and delight. He witnessed them with quiet, "adorational attentiveness"[8] and kept inventory of wonder. For him, the heavens (and the earth, the neighborhood, the forest, the field, the city, the quiet room, even hell itself) declared the glory of God.

A number of the songs I've written—"Everything Is a Fingerprint," "Happy Lightning," "Tap the Kaleidoscope," "Sweetness," "Why Flowers?"—are the result, in large part, of his influence. Whatever clarity of sight I possess, slight as it might be, I owe in large part to spending time with him.

Gary's appreciation of the fingerprints of God was refreshingly simple and plain-spoken. He was an earthy man who thought deeply but spoke simply, a stark and pleasant contrast to those who do it the other way around. He did not need, know, or use arcane words (like his older brother tends to do). If short, common words—like those Jesus used—could express a thought, he shunned any attempt to impress or encumber others with nuance.

And so a sunrise was simply *beautiful.*

A beehive was simply *fascinating.*

An old friend was simply *wonderful.*

God *good.*

Christ *enough.*

And all that he saw, everything he read, every mystery that presented itself to him, and every human achievement or failure that he observed pushed Gary Christ-ward somehow.

He did not dismiss learning, did not disdain education, did not have contempt for academia. Not at all.

What he did question and distrust was the attainment of learning with no anchor in Truth, the sort of learning that makes people proud and self-sufficient rather than humble and small. In keeping with so much of what he read in Scripture, Gary was interested in being wise rather than merely educated. Somewhere he learned a saying that he often quoted: "One does not learn of Christ or read the Bible for *in*formation, but for *trans*formation."

Some of Gary's close friends were people of meager educa-tion—Deacon Shorty Floyd comes to mind—but Gary held them in highest esteem, like those of whom Scripture speaks when it says that God uses "the foolish things of the world to confound the wise."[9]

Love, rather than knowledge—love for God, for others, for creation, and for self—was the impetus and goal of Gary's curi-osity. If intellect could help him excel in living a life of love, he was all for learning. But he was well acquainted with the warning in Scripture that "knowledge puffs up, but love builds up."[10]

IF THERE IS A piece of recorded music that was the signature of the cancer season for us, it is a hymn collection called *Peace Like a River* by singer/songwriter Chris Rice. When Gary was anxious and troubled by dark dreams early on, when he would nap or simply need rest, at night when we'd lay down to sleep—the familiar tunes, softly and simply rendered, were the tonic we reached for. Even now, when I hear the first notes of that record, I am transported, emotionally and memorably, to my last year with Gary

I wrote this letter to Chris Rice, but for some reason, maybe just busyness, I never mailed it:

Dear Chris,

You and I have some friends in common, and we share the same vocation, but I have not had the pleasure of meeting you. I still hold out hope that I will someday. Such an occasion would allow me to say in person what I will attempt to say here in writing.

I am a never-married bachelor with a never-married bachelor brother, Gary. For the past fifteen years or so, I have been a full-time musician. He, for a bit longer than that, has been a missionary serving in a variety of places around the world.

He fills many roles in my life—best friend, hero, mentor, business partner, and when he is stateside, neighbor. I've always assumed that the two of us would grow old together, either here on the acreage where we live in rural Georgia or on some foreign mission field.

A few weeks ago, Gary was diagnosed with an inoperable brain tumor. At fifty-four and remarkably fit, the news was a jolt to a family and a community that deeply love and admire him. For the foreseeable future, his care is center stage in my thoughts and energies. I have canceled all of my travels and concerts so that I can be close to him, a privilege I'd never have asked for, but one for which I am inexpressibly grateful.

My brother loves music. And I've a hunch that the cancer season will be one well served by songs that encourage, inspire, calm, remind, and give hope.

Which brings me to my reason for writing you.

On the day we received news of Gary's diagnosis, he and I, who both own houses on the property here, moved into our parents' house, partly for convenience in the caregiving process, but also because it seemed right to be close together during this time. It looks like we'll be here for a long spell.

On our first night here, Gary and I slept upstairs in an unpartitioned room that serves as a dorm when we have lots of family together. The following morning, very early, I could hear Gary crying, a hard troublesome cry. When I whispered to ask if he was okay, he got out of his bed, walked to my side of the room, and knelt down, sobbing. He had had very dark dreams and was frightened and anxious. I held him while he cried and tried to put his mind at rest.

Thinking afterward that songs might dispel his anxiousness, I turned on *Peace Like a River,* your recording of hymns. I wish, for the sake of encouraging and reminding you of music's power, you could have been here to see the immediate change that came over my brother. His fretfulness lifted, his countenance softened, he breathed peacefully, he rested, and, finally, he slept. Since then, weeks ago now, your songs have been the soundtrack of our rest times and hospital visits. Gary asks for them and recognizes them immediately. They take him to a good place, a God place.

In our second night at our parents' house, instead of sleeping far across the room from Gary as I had the night before, I moved to a single bed—"little boy beds" we call them—beside the one that Gary had chosen to sleep in. There is only about three feet of space between them. If Gary became restless, or cried, or was in need of anything during the night, I was close enough to hear and respond immediately.

We both read, prayed together, and talked before we turned off the lights that night. When the room finally did go dark, your voice was the one that stilled our hearts and sang us into silence. Before giving way to sleep, my brother and I, as we always do when we're together, said our "love yous" and "see you in the mornings." But something more this time. We reached across the dark, that little three-foot space, and held hands. At least for that moment, we were consciously and deeply grateful that we had been given one more day together, and that regardless of what might come tomorrow, our hope was unending. I am sure we both cried ourselves to sleep that night.

And all the while, your kind, gentle voice was there, holding out words of promise.

I imagine that some, or much, of the work you do—writing, practicing, reflecting, wrestling with words—is done in solitude, away from rooms full of listeners, in spaces and in seasons that might make you wonder sometimes if any of it matters, if anyone's listening.

I'm writing to say that someone is, with profound gratitude, and to great benefit.

A fifty-four-year-old saint of God is taking his final steps in this world, celebrated and surrounded by a host of others who can barely imagine life without him. You, Chris, are helping us all, Gary and us, to walk these steps with grace and certainty.

What you do matters.

Just wanted you to know that. And to say thank you.

> With peace like a river,
> —allen

FOR TWO OR THREE years before Gary became ill, whenever he was home from Afghanistan, he and I attended Longstreet Baptist Church, about three miles east of the farm on Highway 208. The building is plain and inconspicuous. The congregation is small, neighborly, and entirely, except for the two of us, African American.

My first visit to Longstreet Baptist came in response to an invitation from Deacon Benjamin "Shorty" Floyd, an elderly man who was a long-time neighbor and friend of our family. He lived in a humble dwelling, a shack really, about two miles east of us and was an officer and icon at Longstreet, the church he attended from 1943 until he passed away in 2011. When I first visited—much to his surprise, I think—I had no idea it would become my regular place of Sunday congregational worship, which it remains to this day.

The music at Longstreet consists largely of old, old spirituals. Many of the songs we sing are done *a cappella*, led by a deacon or deacons. There is a lot of repetition, and the verses are often nearly identical. The melodies include lots of drones, moans, bent notes, and trills, vocal modes I find beautiful, haunting, and evocative. Those sounds—the non-lyric—seem to pick up where the words leave off. I often think they are a truer expression of our hearts than the parts of the songs we understand. Even now, I rarely attend a service when the music doesn't bring tears to my eyes.

WHEN GARY BECAME TOO weak to walk anymore, we had a hospital bed set up on the porch on the west side of Mom and Dad's house. The porch has large plate glass windows that overlook the pond, the pastures, and the tree line. Placing Gary there meant that during his last weeks and days, he was surrounded by sights and sounds that were comforting to him—songbirds, spring and summer foliage, glorious sunsets, starlight, and night music. There were regular visits, usually very short, from friends who would sit beside the bed to hold Gary's hand, to talk and pray with him. Someone from the family was always nearby in case he needed anything.

As we had been told would happen, Gary grew weaker and weaker during the last weeks of his life. He spoke less and less and showed all the signs that the cancer was growing and claiming more and more of his faculties. The family tightened the circle around him, remained vigilant, and sought any little way that we might help or express our love to Gary as he trickled away from us.

Till the end, he was responsive to touch and to sound. The calming effect that came over him whenever someone touched him—took his hand, stroked his face, rubbed his feet or shoulders—was palpable. We consciously made sure that when we were beside him—which was always—we maintained physical contact to assure him of our presence.

Music, as long as it was soft and slow, had the same visible effect as touch. We learned from the medical people that hearing is the last sense to leave a dying body. And so, as Gary's passing drew nearer, it became my habit to pull a chair close beside the bed, drop the guard rail, take Gary's hand, lay my head close to his, and begin to sing. I sang songs of Longstreet, two in particular, songs that I could sing for hours: one, "Come and Go to That Land," and the other, "Since I Laid My Burden Down."

"Singing" might be the wrong word. In truth, it was closer to a tuned whisper, a musical drone, hardly audible unless, like Gary, one was inches away. I don't know that he paid attention to or understood the words, but I believe he was glad for my nearness and reckoned himself safely among those who loved him. His face, when he was fully silent and barely responsive, was strangely beautiful—to all appearances unworried and peaceful.

By the time Gary became sick, I had been a full-time vocational musician for a decade and a half. I had played a wide variety of venues and for all manner of audience. I had seen the way songs can work on peoples' minds and emotions. I had received consistent affirmation, had enjoyed a steady diet of work without ever seeking or soliciting it, and had reason to believe that music was my calling in life.

I pray that I have used that talent for noble ends—to provoke God-ward thought, to celebrate the fullness of life that faith in Christ has given me, and to tell the Story by which people can know peace with God and power over death. For as long as I sing, play, and write songs, I hope those ends will continue to guide me.

But regardless of where music takes me, I will never perform for any higher purpose nor any greater audience than when I sang to Gary in his final days and hours. I've wondered if the thousands of creative days prior to that—the concerts, the practicing, the writing—were not simply rehearsal for those days in July 2012. The supreme musical honor of my life was singing to a man who couldn't walk, couldn't see, couldn't speak. To an audience that slept and whose ovation was silence.

OVER THE YEARS, GARY was an enthusiastic supporter of the musical work I've done. He was always quick to offer words of affirmation and frequently told stories of how he had used one of my songs or recordings in his work as a missionary. It was not unusual to hear my voice singing over the loudspeakers wired throughout the rooms and onto the front porch of his house. Could there be any finer tribute to a singer's work than that?

He reminded me often that the talent for music, like any other talent, was a trust, a gift, a matter of stewardship rather than self-promotion.

Gary was, by nature, an encourager. It was one of the things that made him so pleasant to be around. As a volunteer at the local elementary school, he was quick to applaud the stumbling efforts of a child learning to read. At the high school, he would show up at sporting events—girls' softball, boys' wrestling, volleyball, baseball, and others in which he had meager interest and little or no understanding—just for the chance to pat a kid on the back. He regularly went to school plays, band concerts, and choral performances in hopes of encouraging teachers and students in those programs. He offered words of praise to those who excelled in academics and language and community service.

For years, Gary gave a scholarship out of his own pocket to a student who exemplified Christian service and character. He named it after Mom, "The Hilda Levi Christian Service Award." It was presented each year at the annual awards banquet, which was typically attended by hundreds from the community. He took special pleasure in being able to use the name of Christ, without reprisal, in explaining the criteria for the award. "This award is given to a student who has consistently and visibly been a witness for Christ and the gospel during the school year." His hope on that occasion was to embolden students to stand with conviction for their faith, to honor Christ, and to love others in Christ's name.

In that same spirit of encouragement, Gary began a ritual that became a fixture in my life.

Whenever he was home from overseas, he always knew my travel schedule. He didn't always know exactly *where* I was going, but he always knew *when* I was going somewhere to play. On my departure days he would inevitably show up at my house or at the studio to send me off. He would say a prayer and ask a blessing for my trip. The prayers were predictably hopeful, kind, and thankful—hopeful in reminding me that God had always used weak instruments, broken people, imperfect words, and even simple songs to tell the gospel of Jesus; kind in acknowledging my practice or preparation for the trip at hand; thankful in expressing his gratitude for our brotherhood and friendship.

The prayers most frequently took place beside my truck, usually after my guitars and bags were stuffed into the back seat and ready to go. Gary always put his arm around my shoulder. I always put mine around his. We always hugged after the prayer, always said we loved each other.

I travel now without those prayers, without that simple ceremony of departure. I miss it. Perhaps, though, he knows my schedule even now and still prays hopeful, kind, thankful prayers on my behalf.

It is my new practice, when I leave the farm for music travels, to stop at the cemetery beside the chapel, to sit or kneel,

to pray. I touch the grass above his heart. I tell him I love him.
And I always ask that what I sing and say to my listeners might
be the sorts of things that would bring gladness to him.

Laugh

IF YOU WERE TO ask anyone who knew Gary well for a list of his defining characteristics, everyone would include laughter. Any list without it would be clear proof that the person making it had not spent much time around him.

It is the thing I miss most about his daily presence—those times that he would share a story or describe something in his own colorful way, or use a phrase or point out something in a public place that he knew would appeal to our quirky sense of humor. Laughter featured prominently in the language of our friendship. We used it a lot.

And anywhere Gary went—ask anyone who knew him—laughter went as well. Not the cynical, mean-spirited, sarcastic kind that appeals to the worst in us, but the spontaneous, irresistible sort that flows from and brings out the better angels of our nature.

Now, almost a year since Gary's passing, I realize that when he was taken from our family, there were parts of us each that he took with him. I don't laugh at all like I used to. Can't. The experiences we shared, the language we cultivated, and the lens through which we viewed the world had shaped a key, one of a kind, and placed it exclusively in his hand. It fit my humor in a way that none other does and opened the room where my deepest laughter lived—the kind that is immediate, unguarded, invigorating, and sincere. And nothing made Gary laugh like making someone else laugh.

GARY'S SENSE OF HUMOR was not comedic. He didn't tell jokes. He wasn't silly or wisecrack funny. Crude humor made him blush more than laugh. He didn't *try* to be funny or make things up to get a laugh out of others. His sense of humor was, for lack of a better term, situational. Watching real people doing real things, unscripted and innocently, was his favorite form of entertainment.

He *could* be a prankster at times, but always in well-mannered ways. He was a great fan of *Candid Camera* in the day.

The best way to describe Gary's sense of humor is to tell you some of the things that made him laugh.

He loved to tell the story about his hike on the Appalachian Trail when he was in college. It would begin with Gary describing how his lifelong friend, Mac Turner, showed up for the hundred-mile hike with two six-packs of canned Coca-Cola, the ideal ration for someone who was about to walk the most difficult stretch of the A.T. in a brand-new, just-out-of-the-box, never-worn pair of hiking boots. Two minutes into the story, a story I heard dozens of times, usually at my instigation, we would both be in tears with laughter. Gary always told it as if he just gotten home from the trail yesterday.

It was one of Dad's favorite stories too.

Then there was the story he would tell about an acquaintance of ours who put on an electric dog collar to see how strong the shock was. Answer: strong enough to knock the fillings out of one's teeth.

And he loved to watch Mick Jagger dance. Gary could not tell you the names of five songs by the Rolling Stones, but he would howl at the sight of Jagger dancing—gyrations that Gary considered prime material for a "Don't Do Drugs" commercial.

There was also the occasion when Gary visited me in Scotland. We had supper one night with a friend of mine from China. Wei was an opera singer, Chinese style—very theatrical, relying heavily on gesture, body language, dance, and facial expression. He really could be over the top.

It might well be that Wei was quite accomplished and legit as a singer. I honestly don't know. The art form is jarring to an American with no background in Chinese opera. I knew Gary would find it—well, I'm not sure what I thought Gary would make of it. I just knew I wanted him to experience it. And I knew I wanted to be there when he did.

After we had eaten, I asked Wei if he would sing us a song, something he was all too happy to do. Of course, I knew what was coming. Gary did not have a clue.

In tribute to our cultural roots, Wei announced that he would sing "Way Down Upon the Suwannee River" by Stephen

Foster. He sang in what might best be described as "Chinglish." If he'd not told us the song title, I doubt Gary or I either one would have been able to name that tune.

At the first few notes, and following a couple of gestures that would have made Mick Jagger envious, Gary caught my eye as if to say, "This *is* a joke, isn't it? This is really a prank, *right?*"

It was neither.

It was a serious performance, which meant that: 1) it was way funnier than it would ever have been as intentional comedy, and 2) we could not laugh. With each extreme gesture and every shrill note—all of the notes, by the way, in Wei's rendition of the song fell somewhere on the shrill spectrum—I could see something like a small shock, dog collar-esque, run through Gary as he tried not to laugh. He was like a man holding back a sneeze or trying to keep volleyballs underwater.

Gary and I both knew that eye contact with one another was out of the question. International relations were at stake. And so we mostly looked at our hands or closed our eyes, to convey the sense of rapture I'm sure Wei wanted us to experience at that operatic moment.

Whenever Wei *did* make eye contact with Gary, as good performers will do to connect with their audiences, I could tell that Gary's thoughts were somewhere between "I can't believe this is happening to me" and "This is the greatest moment of my life."

I don't know how Gary and I kept it together, but we did, all the "way dong upong the Shrawny Rivull."

Real life. The funniest thing of all.

MOM AND DAD GREW up during the Depression years. They were children in the 1930s, and the deprivation of that period in American history left a mark on them, as it seems to have done on the collective psyche of their entire generation. They believed in hard work. And did it. And they made sure their five children were familiar with it too.

The first real job Gary and I had was that of paper boy. That job is now a relic of the past. It dates me and under-scores how much the world has changed since Gary and I were kids.

Every day, except Sundays, Gary and I delivered the evening newspaper, the *Columbus Ledger-Enquirer*, to subscribers in our neighborhood, about 150 of them. We were twelve or thir-teen years old, which meant we did the delivery by bicycle. Newspapers for the day were dropped off at our house on Carson Drive in bundles. We untied the bundles, folded the papers individually, put rubber bands on them, and loaded them onto our bikes. If the day was rainy or wet, we had the added responsibility of putting the newspapers in plastic bags. We then rode to the houses on our route and threw the papers onto driveways or porches.

On Sundays we were required to deliver the papers in the morning, before sunrise—rain, sun, sleet, or snow.

We learned quickly where all the bad dogs were, and how to avoid them. And the bad customers, the ones who were generous with complaints and stingy with payments.

Our neighborhood was considerably hilly. We charted a route to take advantage of gravity as much as possible. The work kept us healthy and embarrassingly skinny. And there was a competitive element to it as we tried to outpace each other and be the first back to the house each day.

Once every three months we had to go to every customer—door to door—to collect subscription fees. I think we both learned then, through the disappointing examples of our elders, to be prompt with bill payments and, when possible, lavish with tips.

We threw that paper route for a year or two.

Every summer after that, and usually during the school year too, we had paying jobs—at the sod farm, at Callaway Gardens, at the Pepsi warehouse, at a clothing store, with a pulpwood crew, in construction, and at sundry other places where young men with little skill can make themselves useful. Our jobs were rarely indoors, and they were always minimum wage.

Every job introduced us to memorable, salt-of-the-earth souls and sometimes to entire summers filled with laughter.

Here's another example of the kind of good natured, unrehearsed moment that Gary witnessed with considerable glee:

In our part of the country, there is a lizard that locals call the "scalyback." There is probably a more scientific name, but that's all I've ever heard it called. A scalyback looks a bit like a miniature dinosaur—a hideous concoction of grays and blacks, with a beady-eyed face and blue patches on its undersides. They are extremely fast, frighteningly snakish, and as harmless as fresh air.

I've learned that if conversation slows down among small-town Southern men—say, over breakfast and coffee at the local eatery—it can always be revitalized by the mere mention of snakes. "Man, I nearly stepped on a rattlesnake yesterday" gets almost as spirited a response as "Man, did y'all hear what the Senate just voted to spend money on?" Snakes is the more preferable of the two topics because it doesn't make anyone mad and because snakes are, at least in small-town diners, more highly thought of than senators.

Once snakes become the topic of talk, everyone tells his story or stories of the near bite, or the biggest one (which always involves the phrase "as big as my thigh"), or the one that swam at you with its head up out of the water while you were fishing, or the one you encountered under the crawlspace of the house when you were on your belly checking out the air conditioning ductwork, or the one that climbed straight up a wall and simply disappeared while you went to find a shovel to hit it with. I've got some snake stories of my own (in addition to the ones I borrow from other survivors) and proudly defend my status as probably the only musician in the country who has killed a rattler *inside* his recording studio. (It happened in the same year that, unbeknownst to me, a nest of them lived right outside my door.)

Summer is always the snaky time of year. Those who work outdoors in the country learn to be cautious about where they step from May through October. Small, crooked sticks and dead branches that lie all over the forest floor and bear striking resemblance to reptiles give one's adrenal glands a healthy workout over the course of a day. Though I can no longer move with the speed I had when I was younger, my reflexes are still pretty impressive when I encounter a stick pretending to be a snake. After such encounters, I always look around to make sure no one has seen me when I have just leapt with superhuman quickness to elude a life-threatening, four-foot-long, "big as my thigh" piece of tree wood.

During one summer in high school, Gary and I worked on a nearby sod farm. We were stacking hay with a black guy named Robert, a guy just a few years older than our fifteen or sixteen years. (I hope you don't mind my use of the term "black guy." That's what we—black and white—are most comfortable with around here. My friends of color, including Deacon Floyd, have told me that "black" is the term they want me to use. I have asked around, out of a desire to be considerate, and the answer has always been the same. They call men like me "white guys," and I use the term "black guy" when necessary. No pretense. No meanness. The terms can be said, and are, with kindness and love. They work.) Robert had the most heartfelt, enthusiastic laughter I think I've ever heard. For him, laughing was a full-body, lung-depleting, lip-stretching, tear-inducing experience that happened multiple times a day. The hot, demanding work of the sod farm was largely made endurable and enjoyable by the simple presence of Robert's joviality.

We had been stacking bales of hay in a small, wooden barn-like structure. Think weather-beaten boards and rusty tin roof. It was midmorning, and any coolness that might have welcomed the day was long gone. We'd been working several hours and were taking a break, sitting on some of the hay bales. Somebody brought up the topic of snakes; I don't recall who. My guess is that mention was made of how snakes sometimes get caught up in the hay by the baling machine. Stories followed. It became obvious that Robert shared, in fact considerably surpassed, my fear of snakes. There was not much laughter in the conversation. Instead, there were consistent expressions of disbelief.

"You fuh-real?"

"Ain't no way."

"Huh-UH."

"Come on."

The more snake-infested our thoughts became, the more our stories strayed from the truth. For the rest of the day, we would all be on the lookout for serpents in the field. Snake conversation has the power to put you on edge and make you skittish.

You cannot imagine the display of reactive shock, the sheer explosion of nerves, the man-shot-out-of-a-cannon energy released when, in the middle of our snake talk, a scaly-back lizard jumped from a barn rafter into Robert's hair. His response was as immediate, as vocal, as uncontrolled, and as expressive as anything I've ever beheld. I don't know if Robert actually knew what had happened, or whether he simply detected a look of terror in my face and Gary's, but it was clear that he thought he had just been attacked by a flying snake.

With lightning speed, he began to run—why or where is beyond me—swatting his head, screaming and jumping with the handwork of a helicopter and the footwork of an ice-skater, making sounds I'd never heard before and haven't heard since.

I have no idea where that scalyback lizard ended up, but my guess is that it lived in mortal fear of barns for the rest of its days.

When the episode had passed, we all—Robert most of all—howled with laughter.

I rarely see a scalyback lizard without remembering that day. And I don't think Gary did either.

Real life. The best entertainment.

A final bit of advice: If snakes don't liven up the conversation, try yellow jackets.

IN 1978, A FEW summers after the sod farm experience, Gary and I worked at Dad's sawmill. We were both in college by then; Gary was an undergraduate, and I had just finished my four-year degree at the University of Georgia. I would have been 22, he 20, when the summer began. It was the summer before I started law school.

As a timber buyer, Dad purchased tracts of timber (trees still in the forest, to be cut down) that would be harvested and delivered to his sawmill. There the trees were cut into boards (lumber). The boards were then sold for use in construction or manufacturing.

Dad's first mill was a small one located on the Hamilton/ Pleasant Grove Road, four miles east of the farm. It gave him the chance to test the market and assess his ability to run such a business. The mill proved successful, and a few years later he built a much bigger one in Shiloh, Georgia.

The summer of 1978, Gary and I mostly worked the green chain—a conveyor belt from which fresh-cut boards had to be removed by hand and stacked according to size. All day long we pulled the boards off of the conveyor and placed them in their appropriate stacks. They varied in dimension, from two-by-four up to six-by-six and were different lengths. The green chain provided me with a keen incentive to do well in law school, which was exactly what Dad had in mind when he put me there.

A day at the sawmill meant noise (the deafening whine of the saw), dirt (dust, grease, and sweat), and heat (summer in Georgia). But it was good, honest, invigorating work.

That was the year Gary and I met Mr. Maddox, an older worker, sixty or so, who had been with Dad for a number of years. Mr. Maddox operated the saw, slowly but well.

He was a smallish man with sleepy eyes and a slow gait. He seemed incapable of hurry. We would learn over the course of the summer that he was somewhat superstitious and slightly gullible. He spoke in short phrases with a sing-song voice, high and thin. One of the phrases he used that became a permanent part of our vocabulary was "right is right." It doesn't rise to the level of "Ihehyabah" (more about that shortly), but it got frequent usage over the years, usually as part of a more complete thought—"You know you wrong, Bah, right is right."

As the summer progressed, Mr. Maddox began losing the teeth on one side of his mouth. He explained to us during lunch one day that he was planning to get dentures, and first, his permanent teeth had to be removed. He underwent those extractions a few at a time as he had money to pay for them. The dentist apparently did not pull teeth on credit.

Once Mr. Maddox had gotten half of his teeth pulled— the top and bottom right side—the process stopped. We asked him what had happened—such a question is not considered impolite or too personal when you've worked in a sawmill together—and he explained that he wanted to replace some shingles on his house, which meant delaying the dentures until he got the roof finished.

That decision had a noticeable effect on Mr. Maddox's face. One cheek developed a sunken-ness about it, which made him an absolute hazard to sit beside at mealtime. His eating became an unfortunate combination of chew and spray, especially when he spoke with a full mouth—another practice comfortably within the bounds of sawmill etiquette. It took an artful dodger to escape the debris of his lunch. Certain words—mostly those with plosives like b, d, p, or t—could lead to a spray that can only be described as volcanic. We quickly learned which side of Mr. Maddox was safest to sit on and what minimum distance it was prudent to maintain whenever we ate lunch with him.

Once his roofing decision was final, Mr. Maddox had no more teeth removed that summer. It did not seem to bother him at all.

That same summer, one of Gary's closest friends, Mac Flowers, worked at the mill with us. He too worked the green chain, but since he had experience with heavy equipment, he often operated the front-end loader and forklift as well.

A few years previous, Mac had been involved in a serious automobile accident from which he escaped with relatively little injury. He sustained some cuts, though, and had a bit of minor scarring on his face.

One day while Mac was elsewhere in the yard, his accident became the topic of lunchtime conversation. The details of the accident—how it happened, where it happened, how much damage was done to the car, who got in trouble, what a miracle it was that no one was killed—were thoroughly gone over.

Mr. Maddox listened with rapt attention. He said little but did ask questions from time to time. At the more spectacular details—"They hit that parked car going fifty miles an hour!"—Mr. Maddox would shake his head and respond through his closed mouth with a very appropriate "uh-uh-uh."

Then the story took a fictitious turn.

Me: "You know they had to do a special operation on Mac's face."

Mr. Maddox: "Did?"

Me: "Oh yeah, his cheek was torn up real bad—where that scar is now—and some of the meat came out of it."

Mr. Maddox, a bit more emphatically: "*Did?*"

Me: "So what they did was, the doctor took a shot and filled it up with some kind of plastic stuff and put it in Mac's cheek and then sewed it up so it would look kind of normal. But his whole cheek on that side is pretty much just made out of plastic."

Mr. Maddox, totally fascinated and horrified to know that he had been working for a month alongside Frankenstein, became downright eloquent: "UH-UH-UH."

Then Gary got involved.

"One of the things Mac has to be careful about is not to get too hot. The doctor told him if he gets too hot, the side of his face might melt. If Mac ain't careful, his whole cheek will just melt down into his jaw."

Mr. Maddox is thunderstruck. For a fraction of a second, we could actually see the white of his eyes.

"That's why Mac goes to the water bucket so much. You watch him. He'll go into the tool room so he can get in the shade and splash water on this face. That's how he cools it down so it won't melt. Next time he goes in the tool room, you just watch."

"Uh-uh-uh."

"But whatever you do, don't say anything to him about it. And don't let him catch you looking at him. He's kind of sensitive about it, and if he catches somebody gazing at him, it really upsets him. Sometimes he just sort of goes crazy."

"Duz?"

"Oh yeah. And I tell ya, hot as it's been lately, I been worried about him sweating so much and doing all this hot work. If you ever see him pushing that cheek or holding it with his hand, he's trying to keep it from melting down into his jaw."

Mr. Maddox was gobsmacked. "Uh-uh-uh."

When Gary and I talked with Mac later that day, we told him about the medical procedure he had been through and instructed him to make sure that, going forward, he put his hand to his face—the plastic side—from time to time.

For additional entertainment value, we made the suggestion to Mac that whenever he saw Mr. Maddox go to the water bucket in the tool room, he ought to follow and stand as close to him as possible, preferably close enough to make some bodily contact.

From then on, Mr. Maddox approached Mac as if he were a mad dog. If he saw Mac coming toward him, his gaze immediately went to the ground, and he returned to the sawyer's chair with all the fervor of a child going to Disneyland.

Imagine our delight when Mr. Maddox told us one day he thought he had seen "some of that plastic stuff coming out of Mac's face."

Gary and I lost touch with Mr. Maddox after that summer. We don't know if he ever got his dentures or finished his roof. But we never remembered him without paying him the high compliment of our best laughter.

GARY'S HUMOR COULD BE insightfully clever at times.

Someone gave me a bumper sticker that is on display in my studio. It bears the following text:

> Simplify, simplify.
> —Henry David Thoreau

When Gary first saw it, he walked over to my desk, got a piece of paper, wrote something down, and then took it and taped it to the bottom of Thoreau's quote. It read simply:

> Simplify.
> —Gary Levi

As GARY GREW WEAKER, due in large part to medicines he was taking, his recreational activities decreased. The same strong legs that had made bicycling one of Gary's favorite pastimes began to lose muscle mass, so much so that hikes in the woods soon became short walks on the road, which soon became even shorter strolls on the circular gravel driveway around the house, a distance of about three hundred yards. And even those walks got shorter and shorter, from several laps, to one, to none. When he *did* walk—or shuffle—someone always had to be with him, and he often used a walking stick to steady himself. We learned it was helpful to lock an elbow with Gary or to have a handhold on his belt in case he lost his balance. It was usually necessary to pause every now and then so that he could catch his breath.

Those slow walks, like others from healthier days, were where we had some of our best conversations.

And some of our best cancer season laughter.

On one occasion, midmorning on a clear day, Gary and I were about two-thirds of the way around the driveway when either he told me or I sensed that he was getting dizzy and losing control of his legs. Increasingly, there were instances when, without warning, Gary would get wobbly. "Go jello" we called it.

It became obvious to me that our walk was over. Problem was, we still had about seventy-five yards to go.

I turned to face Gary, put my arms around him and his around me. I walked backward slowly, and he did his best to follow. His feet were not cooperative, so I essentially dragged him to the house in choppy, unsteady, awkward steps.

Shortly into that process, we tried to imagine what we must look like and what strangers would think if they saw us at that moment.

"Bah, I hope nobody drives up right now."

That got us laughing. And something about laughing made us laugh even harder until we were laughing in the way that takes your breath away and brings water to your eyes. And every choppy, unsteady, awkward step made it worse. We had become effectively one body with four legs, chest to chest and cheek to cheek, and that element of proximity added fuel to our laughter.

We would later call it "The Drunkard's Dance." We were two drunks on a Saturday night, sliding around the dance floor with all the gracefulness of first-time roller skaters.

After that, whenever Gary would go jello, I knew what to ask: "All right, Bah. May I have this dance?"

And dance we did.

THERE IS A PICTURE on the wall in my studio. It's the same picture we used on the program for Gary's memorial service. It is a picture of him and Deacon Floyd, caught in the act of laughing. I had recently finished a record called *People in My Town,* and we were taking pictures for the cover. Deacon Floyd was there because one of the songs on the CD was about him. Gary just happened to stop by. The two of them sat down and started talking. I have no idea what they were saying to one another, but King Davis, the photographer, snapped a rapid sequence of three pictures that caught their laughter as it unfolded.

Often, when I think of Gary, that sequence of images is the one that comes to mind. Head thrown back. Eyes pinched shut with delight. Mouth wide open. Laughter without guile.

FOR MANY YEARS I have been an avid subscriber to and reader of *National Geographic* magazine. I sometimes describe it as one of the most theologically informative pieces of literature that I study—cover to cover—every month. I cannot be confronted with this vast, complex, colorful, orderly, living, energetic, singingly curious creation without thinking, *What sort of glorious God must He be who could make and oversee such a universe?*

I read an article in *National Geographic* during Gary's last summer, shortly after he passed way. The article was about lost languages, about dialects and native tongues that dwindle and disappear when small people-groups lose membership. As the older people pass away, and as the younger assimilate more widespread languages, the household words of those micropopulations die off with them.

It occurred to me that when Gary went silent, a language—ours—was lost. There were phrases, intonations, pronunciations, subtleties, and references that were ours alone. And when Gary left this world, our shared language went with him.

I suppose every marriage, every family, every deep friendship spawns a language like that, a language spoken in the dark and in the daily life of people who are safely known by one another. It is a language as sacred as prayer to those who use it. And it's missed when it's gone.

If you spent any time with me and Gary in recent decades, you were sure to have heard us use a word, or phrase, that had a conspicuous place in our vocabulary—"Ihehyabah." We used it constantly.

"I"

"Heh"

"Ya"

"Bah"

It began with the word "bah" in 1975. That was the year the public schools in Columbus, Georgia (and throughout the South), were desegregated. Our new dark-skinned classmates, six hundred or so (there had been only two the year before), would call each other "boy" in a manner that sounded like little more than the consonant "b." "Bah" was how we heard it.

"Ihehya" was added to our lexicon in 1978. That was the summer that Gary and I worked at the sawmill with Mr. Maddox. There was another employee there: Edwin—a tall, lanky guy twice our age who had a girlfriend he called "Popeye." "Ihehya" was his phrase. As a greeting, as an all-purpose rejoinder (in the way that some folks will use "okay" or "unh-hunh" to fill pauses in a conversation), as a way of expressing any emotion, Edwin would say, "I hear you"— only, it came out southernized as "I heh ya." It was not three single-syllable words but one three-syllable word, adaptable to a myriad of uses.

"Good morning, Edwin," I'd say.

Edwin would answer, "I heh ya." (Said with a hand wave, cheerfully and energetically.)

I'd say, "Man, it's hot today, isn't it?"

Edwin would say, "I heh ya." (Said with a shake of the head and appropriate weariness.)

I'd ask, "Edwin, can you grab that chain for me?"

"I heh ya, " he replies, hurriedly and with little inflection.

"Edwin, Mr. Steve wants you at the office."

"I heh ya." (Said with tilted head and a tone of apprehension. Mr. Steve was the boss man.)

"Edwin, good gosh, man, be more careful with that chain saw."

"I HEH yaa." (All anger and disgust.)

"Edwin, you gonna take Popeye on a date this weekend?"

"I hehhhya." (Drawn out long and slow, with smile on face and twinkle in eye.)

So Gary and I joined 1975 and 1978 together and came up with a phrase that I would conservatively estimate we used ten times a day throughout our adult lives. "Ihehyabah."

When Gary wrote me letters or emails, they almost always began, "Dear Bah." I have sung "Ihehyabah" in a number of songs I've recorded. When Gary and I were together with others, they often asked us what we were saying whenever they heard us use the phrase. ("Are y'all calling each other Bob?") Very few ever tried to use it themselves.

Other phrases—"Settalegs and the wild continuous party," "Pipeline," "What's-the-matter-Jimmy-can'tcha-do-yah-job," "Don't shout me down," "Big Lou," "Call Johnny

Harris"—all have origins and associations of their own.

I mourn their extinction.

The lost language of the brothers Levi.

PERHAPS, IN TRIBUTE TO Gary, we can keep one small part of that language alive—this one: Settalegs and the wild continuous party. It is a nonsensical bit of my and Gary's history, but I'll bet when you saw the phrase three paragraphs ago, you wondered what it was about, didn't you? It's kind of catchy. Maybe even song material.

We were on a family vacation at the beach in Destin, Florida. Gary and I were teenagers. You know how it is when you go to the beach and stay for a week? You see some of the same people every day, either because they're staying in the unit beside yours or because they set up their beach umbrellas next to you in the sand each morning. By the end of the week, you know each other on a first name basis. Then there are others you don't actually meet, but you see them enough to recognize their faces.

One of the faces that we saw each day on that particular vacation belonged to a guy from Memphis. My educated guess is that he was twenty, and he belonged to a fraternity at a college where he was on academic probation, and he was being groomed to take over the family business or go into politics. At any time after eleven in the morning, he always had a beer in his hand and a boast on his tongue. He was outgoing, loud, highly watchable, and, to Gary and me, likeable. Wherever he was—at the seaside, by the pool, or on his balcony—he was angling to be the center of attention. He seemed convinced that everyone on that beach had come to the Florida panhandle just for the opportunity to meet him. And he was there to oblige us all.

Gary and I spoke with him a time or two, or more precisely, listened to him. Settalegs did not have much interest in voices other than his own. We determined quickly that he ranked low on the credibility meter but high on the entertainment scale.

We never got his name. So we had to come up with some way to identify him, something that we could use for our conversational purposes later on. He was tall, and the architecture of his body was striking. His legs seemed to make up a disproportionate part of his height. He was like a house built on stilts. Most folks' bodies are about half above the waist and half below. This guy was about one-third/two-thirds. He had a long set of legs.

Hence, the name.

"Did you see old Settalegs trying to talk to those girls from Auburn down by the pool?"

"Yeah, did you notice how they all suddenly had an urge to go swimming in the ocean?"

He was at his most entertaining when he was attempting flirtation. I don't think he had any idea just how bad he was at it. The girls reacted to his approach the same way Mr. Maddox did whenever Mac Flowers entered the tool room at the sawmill. The word "evacuate" comes to mind. But Settalegs was never disheartened; he stayed in pursuit mode all week long. The more bothersome he was to the girls, the more watchable he was to me and Gary.

I wish I could tell you that he actually did something notable that week—that he rescued a beautiful girl from a rip tide, or raised money for the Audubon Society, or had a scalyback jump into his beer—but there was nothing of the sort. He just hung around and talked a lot and put on lots of suntan oil.

On the last day of his vacation, Settalegs honored us with a sort of farewell speech. There were a number of people on the ground floor parking lot when, out of the blue, he started addressing no one in particular but everyone within earshot.

"Well, folks, it has been good being with y'all. We're getting ready to head on back to Memphis. If y'all ever get up that way, y'all look me up, and we will just have us *a wild continuous party*. Yessir, a wild continuous party!"

And with that, Settalegs and his traveling companion got into a high-dollar convertible, spun the tires, and tore out across the parking lot, Memphis bound.

I don't know why Gary and I found that so funny or memorable, but we did. Decades later, he and I might be riding down the road, not talking for a long stretch, when one of us would break the silence,

"Bah"—long pause—"whatcha' reckon Settalegs is doing right now?"

"Bah, he's up there in Memphis, Tennessee, having a wild continuous party."

And, guaranteed, we'd laugh.

Crazy, the things we remember.
Crazy, the things I miss.

THERE WAS A CURIOUS and funny thing that Gary and Dad used to do. I'm sure there must be a picture of it somewhere. They would tease each other about something, bantering in *their* own language (Dad was also one of the Bah membership), and strike a pose that, to me, became a trademark of their friendship. Gary would stand an arm's length away from Dad, facing him. He would put both hands on Dad's shoulders, and Dad would put his on Gary's. And they'd talk, picking at each other good-naturedly the whole time. They would lean into each other—imagine a capital letter *A*—and almost, or actually, touch foreheads. The banter would continue accompanied by a constant exchange of laughter.

Those exchanges, body language included, were a part of their vocabulary.

"Missing" is something that can't be quantified. We all do it in our own unique ways and for our own unique reasons. But I don't know that anyone misses Gary's presence more than Dad.

Some months after Gary's passing, Beth found a film that Gary had made years earlier at a family gathering. In the film, Gary is behind the camera, taping Dad. They are engaged in a light-hearted exchange, meaningless to anyone but themselves. After a few moments, Dad tells Gary to turn off the camera. "No, Bah, I am not going to turn it off." Gary is laughing.

Dad is laughing too, at first naturally and then a bit nervously, trying all the while to escape the lens. It is a moment I am fairly certain no one would find funny but them.

Beth brought that film to the farm shortly after she found it. She put it on the television for us to watch. Dad saw himself on the screen and heard Gary—the pre-cancer, healthy, good-humored Gary. The Gary that had been absent for a long time.

Dad began to laugh. And then to cry.

The laughter was of the sort that only Gary could evoke from him. His "Gary laugh." It was the first time I had heard that sound since Gary's passing.

And the tears? I don't know if they were glad tears of remembrance, hopeful tears of missing, irrepressible tears of joy, or plain and simple grief.

At that moment, more than at any time since Gary's passing, I realized how much we all missed him, and how much our worlds had been diminished by his absence.

I don't know what heaven will be like.

The Bible says that it is a place.

I know the Architect and Builder of it.

It was Jesus, after all, who said, "*I go to prepare a place for you.*"

It will surpass the most beautiful and extravagant, the most *National Geographic*, of our imaginations. But if I am allowed to think of it hopefully (and with reference to the present world, which after all is the only world I have to draw from), I do hope I might see Dad and Gary when I get there, leaning into one another, foreheads touching, laughing in that language all their own, their capital A.

Maybe it's just me, but we live in a world full of bad laughter—laughter that is callous, belittling, self-righteous, obscene. Like all the other good gifts that God has given to humanity—food, drink, sex, dominion, language, inventiveness—this one has become tainted through misuse.

But there *is* good laughter; laughter that in some way gives voice to a belief that, in the end, the love of God will prevail over every dark thing. It is the overflow of a soul that has seen, if only slightly, into the heart of Christ. Such laughter has mass to it. It is tethered to something huge and holy. It is the laughter of the ransomed returning home.

It is the sort of laughter that Gary gave away everywhere he went.

IT IS SUMMERTIME AS I write these words. True to my annual habit, I have located the whereabouts of every bird nest in the vicinity of the house: beside the studio, under the barn rafters, and at various and sundry other spots around the farm. For years now, I have taken a paternal interest in the well-being of the songbirds during springtime. The remarkable processes of nesting, gestation (a yolk can turn into that?), incubation, feeding, fledging, and first flight are wondrously entertaining.

I've been intrigued this year by the language of birds—those shrill, metallic screeches of child to parent and parent to child—through which warning, need, hunger, fear, and concern are communicated. And by all accounts, an infant bird in the nest can distinguish from the clamor of morning songs exactly which voice belongs to its mother and father. They all sound mostly alike to me, and yet at one voice only do the young ones go instantly silent when warned, or instantly demanding when in want of attention.

The dialect that Gary and I created unintentionally and shared gladly will always be ours somehow. In a crowd of thousands, let him speak one of those phrases, as only he knows how, and I'd know it immediately. Just like those little birds.

I'd answer it.

Ihehyabah.

Son

In 2008, Dad and Mom, then seventy-nine and eighty, relocated to the farm. They had lived in Columbus, Georgia, till then, about twenty-five miles south of Hamilton. The move meant more work for them. The property, with yards and fields and structures, is relentless in its call for attention. The move meant, too, that their friends and social circle would be a hefty drive away, as would grocery and hardware stores, restaurants and doctors' offices.

On the plus side, the move meant less traffic, less confinement, a bigger sky, and small moments of splendor.

It also meant—and this was their reason for the move— that when Gary was home they'd be closer and able to spend more time with him.

ANYONE WHO LIVED IN the places and endured the challenges that Gary did qualifies as one of irrefutable independence and responsibility. The fact that he was a self-reliant man, though, does not remotely suggest that he ever outgrew his affection for, or his desire to be close to, Dad and Mom.

When people marry, if I read the blueprint correctly, they are counseled, even obligated, to "leave, cleave, and become one." The "leave" part takes place at the wedding altar when they pledge themselves to one another and subordinate (or mysteriously shed altogether) their "son" and "daughter" identities to become "husband and wife." The "cleave and become one" elements are worked out over a lifetime.

"Leave" implies establishment of a new entity, one that is autonomous and responsible for itself. That new entity—a home, a family—will exist in the broader context of extended family and community, but it is separate and entitled to its own identity and space. "Leave" also implies that the parents of the new couple turn loose of them, emancipate them, let them go. We've all seen the damage done when parents of married children don't move out of the way.

"Leave," however, does not mean "disown," "disrespect," or "disregard." It merely indicates that a clear line of demarcation has been drawn between what used to be and what now is.

You're probably wondering, "What's the point?" Especially with regard to Gary.

Well, here's the point. Or maybe the question: How do *unmarried* adult children grow up and "leave" home? Gary and I talked about this from time to time, largely because folks often asked or teased us about the fact that we were two middle-aged men who'd never "committed matrimony" and who still lived near their parents. After all, in cases like ours, there is no formal ceremony, as there is with marriage, that marks the point of separation between parent and child.

For unmarrieds, especially those in their fifties, the relationship to parents can be an uneasy one. I admit that when I hear of single adult children, young or old, living with or very near their parents, it strikes me as a bit unhealthy, as though both parents and children have missed out on a stage of normal adult development. And sometimes I'm right. Other times, though, it just is what it is, and, rightly appreciated, it opens the way for something good, strong, and blessed.

Gary was a good son. He was proud of Dad and Mom and quick to give thanks for his close friendship with them. He gladly acknowledged his indebtedness to them. He knew their faults as well as anyone but loved them devotedly. He even liked them and enjoyed them.

Living as he did, so far and for so long away from friends and family, seemed to have deepened Gary's love for home, true to the adage that absence makes the heart grow fonder. Much of his life was taken up with meeting new people, learning new surroundings, and acclimating to unfamiliar cultures. It's no wonder that when he was stateside and without wife and children to call his family, he found such comfort in being with his siblings, his nieces and nephews, and perhaps most of all, "Dadbo" and "Mombo."

Gary had a daily routine of going to the big house, morning and evening, to check on and visit with Dad and Mom. They didn't require the visits. Even now, in their mid-eighties, they enjoy remarkably good health and are fully capable of independent living. Gary made the short trip—a half mile maybe—simply because he enjoyed their company, as they did his. He was concerned for their happiness and did what he could, including those short visits, to secure it for them.

"Considerate" is a word that I don't hear often these days. It fit Gary well, particularly concerning the kindness he showed to Mom and Dad. Meals he cooked for them, times he took them on outings, his readiness to taxi them on long-distance trips, notes and letters he sent to them, calls home (pre-internet) from far-away places so they could hear his voice and be assured of his well-being, and gifts he brought whenever he returned from overseas were all small evidences of his devotion to them.

That is not to say that the three of them did not disagree or get crossways or impatient with each other at times. Dad and Mom were not exempt from Gary's criticism or correction, nor he from theirs, but the ill effects of such honesty never lasted for long.

Often when we took Gary to the airport for one of his long-term departures, the farewell ritual would include a delivery of letters. Gary would have written each of us a short note in his easily recognizable longhand. If possible, he would place the notes secretly in a book, a coat pocket, or handbag that we might be carrying, trusting that we would find them later on.

Sometimes he would simply place the envelope in our hands immediately before boarding the plane and immediately after it became obvious that we couldn't talk anymore.

The notes were short. They were filled with gratitude and encouragement. They always left us with a lump in the throat.

In time (maybe Mom did it all along), we learned to slip our own notes into his luggage, his book, his coat.

It was a small thing, the writing and exchanging of those bits of paper. I'll bet all of the notes Gary gave to Mom and Dad are somewhere safe in a box, a bag, or a drawer at their house. Mom would have kept them all. Moms do that sort of thing.

God help the ones who have no such items to treasure.

ONE OF THE MOST difficult things about Gary's long last year was witnessing the pain that Mom and Dad carried while they watched his body lose the battle to cancer.

The slow goodbye was hardest on them. They felt, even more than others in the family, the burden of being defenseless against the awful intruder that was taking their son away from them.

They both remained very active during that year. It was their nature. Having grown up poor—her dad was a part-time sharecropper and welder for the Illinois Central Railroad in Mississippi during the Depression—Mom had, still has, an industriousness that does not allow her to sit still for long. Dad, who had managed a sizable work force and dealt daily with the minutiae of running a business, was not one to let the grass grow under his feet either.

They were used to fixing things.

Mom played "food police" and chef when Gary got sick. The food police role did not always meet with his approval. He was quite happy, thank you, with the deep-fried, sugary, large-portioned diet he'd always enjoyed, and he was reluctant to concede that part of his life to cancer. Mom's aim of "going healthy" found a less than enthusiastic target in Gary. She did the best she could.

As resident chef, her work was much more appreciated. Ever the wonderful cook, Mom marshaled her best efforts to assure that Gary ate delicious, if not altogether nutritious, meals. Even after he lost the ability to appreciate how good those meals were, she fed him like royalty.

In the journal I kept, I made a note that along with brain cancer, Gary had contracted a keen interest in cooking shows. When it got harder and harder for him to read or exercise, the Cooking Channel became his main diversion. The sight of Gary, the woodworking outdoorsman, watching petite women and not-so-petite men prepare unpronounceable recipes was a bit incongruous.

Mom often watched the shows with Gary. I think she took a homemaker's pride in knowing that her meals and her attention to detail were no less impressive than what the experts did on television each afternoon.

Late in Gary's illness, but when he was still able to sit up in his wheelchair at the family meal table, Mom was preparing lunch for him one day. By this time, Gary was not eating much. His whole body, stomach included, was giving way to the effects of his illness, and meals had become a necessary habit rather than a source of any discernible pleasure.

I don't recall what the meal was, but I do recall that it was served on fine china. Mom had laid out the portions of food meticulously, elegantly, artfully—as though she were serving a head of state. I had picked up Gary's plate to take it to him at the table. She stopped me, had me put it down, and asked that I go outside to pick some parsley from her small herb garden. Gary's plate would not be complete without that final touch.

I did as I was told.

In better times, Gary might have appreciated that garnish, and he might have recognized it as the gesture of excellence, the nod toward exceptional hospitality, that Mom intended it to be. By now, though, it was a detail that was lost on him.

To Mom, on the other hand, it was simply her way—a small but telling thing. And till the very end, Gary was her honored guest, her beloved son, her little boy, as he had been when all was well. He was royalty till the end.

Sometimes affection is fine as parsley.

As THE DOCTORS TOLD us it would, Gary's condition worsened, little by little. There were days, entire weeks even, when we believed he was beating the cancer. There were other times, which always felt like kicks in the gut, when his reversals were suffocating and undeniable.

Those times were tough for all of us, but especially for Mom and Dad. One stands out to me.

Mom owns a small camera that she hardly knows how to operate. She is only slightly ahead of Dad in her use and understanding of digital technology. But she is a good sport and, unlike Dad, willing to be taught.

We all took pictures of Gary after he got sick, mostly in a desperate but futile attempt to capture and preserve him forever in images. The ones I like best, though, are those I stumble upon accidentally, those from before the cancer, those tucked away in books or other random places, especially the ones that catch him in a candid moment, looking away from the camera; the ones that feel like he's living rather than posing—bending down to pick up a board, opening a jar of honey, reading a newspaper, examining a stump that he's turning on the lathe, laughing at something known only to him. I can't say that I take much pleasure in the pictures we took while he was sick.

Mom took her share of pictures during the early months of his illness. She knew enough about her digital camera to snap images but not enough to do anything with them once they were captured. When the camera memory was full, she asked me to help her "take them off" ("download" was not a term she knew).

On Thanksgiving Day 2011, we downloaded more than 300 pictures and looked at them all, from oldest to most recent. What unfolded before our eyes was a visual diary of a man slowly dying of cancer. The changes in Gary that had been too gradual to notice when they were happening from day to day suddenly became graphically clear when the months could be compressed into a short, chronological slide show.

Mom and I didn't just look at the pictures. We *felt* them. I wished that we, particularly she, had not seen them. Their message was cruel.

IN THE LATE AFTERNOON of the day that we learned of Gary's diagnosis, I heard a low hum in the distance: the familiar and unmistakable sound of the tractor. Dad was mowing the pasture in front of my house.

What he was really doing was working through the news of Gary's tumor. Dad has a great fondness for tractor work and often escapes to the John Deere when, for whatever reason, he wishes to be alone.

Looking back, it doesn't surprise me that, at such a moment, Dad would seek out something familiar and comforting. He knew that if he fired the engine, lowered the bush hog, engaged the power take-off, and pulled forward he would cut a swath in the tall grass and leave something orderly in his wake. The open field, the early evening sky, and the long shadows of sunset were a haven for him at a time when he feared there might be nothing he could humanly engage, no engine that he could fire, and no blade that he could drop in protection of his son.

Who knows what memories might have filled Dad's mind that afternoon? Little boy memories? School day or timber business memories? Travel memories from recent years? Memories of missing him while Gary was away overseas?

THE LAST SWEET MILE

Maybe this one, this one that always made Dad smile, this one that he recounted at Gary's funeral:

The two of them had gone duck hunting in Hurtsboro, Alabama, southwest of Columbus, where one of Dad's clients owned a large piece of timberland. Gary was a little boy—single digits—but clever beyond his years. Dad, with Gary at his side watching and retrieving birds, shot a good number of ducks that afternoon.

The hunt, or the visits afterward with other hunters, lasted longer than Dad had anticipated. He and Gary put their unplucked birds in the car and sped home. Dad and Mom had plans for the evening, and Dad was hurrying to be on time. He looked up to see blue lights in his rearview mirror. A state trooper pulled him over, wrote him a ticket for speeding, and sent him on his way.

Dad, of course, had to say *something* to Gary.

"Now son, I shouldn't have been driving so fast, but look, when we get home, don't you say one word about this to your mother. This is just between us."

Gary got quiet, thought awhile, and then said, "Well if you'll clean the birds, I won't say anything to Mom."

How could a dad not love a boy like that?

As death inched closer and closer to Gary, I think it was harder and harder for Dad to be in his presence. The reality was too unsettling, too close. The air was too thin to breathe. I've a journal entry from one particularly difficult day: "Bad morning. We put Gary to bed and Dad, as he often does, rubs Gary's head, face, temples and says, time and time again, 'My sweet boy.' After Mom and I leave the room, Dad stays behind. Comes out after a few minutes, crying. Leaves the house without a word."

That term of endearment—sweet boy—is Dad's distillation of all Gary was. When I asked him and Mom both, separately, to describe Gary as a child, that was the word they both chose—"sweet." There was nothing pitying or condescending about the term. There was nothing about it that hinted at weakness. It was simply a dad's proud and affectionate acknowledgment that his son was a doer of good, a bringer of gladness, a channel of blessing—a sweet boy.

IF THERE *WAS* A gift to Mom and Dad that came with the year of Gary's illness—and I have to believe that God had many in mind—it might have been this: They had the rare privilege of watching a child finish well. It was a bittersweet privilege for sure, and painful, but it was joyous too.

All the distances that people traveled to be with Gary when he was sick, the letters and calls and gifts that were sent or placed or given in gratitude for his influence in their lives, the outpouring of emotion that characterized so many of his last encounters, and the focus that Gary maintained till the end—on loving the right things—could not prove more convincingly that the son of A. C. and Hilda Levi was a man well-loved because of a life well-lived. That Dad and Mom had brought him into the world and raised him and trained him up, that they had played so large a part in shaping the man that he became—all of that, I trust, while not compensating for their loss, did bring them a measure of peace.

Gary had run a fifty-five-year race, and they were there to watch him running through the tape at the finish.

> The father of a righteous man has great joy;
> he who has a wise son delights in him.
> May your father and mother be glad;
> may she who gave you birth rejoice!
> —Proverbs 23:24–25 NIV

Sadness

In the late 1990s, Gary and four other men met to pray for every kid in the local high school. It was their concern that there might be young people in the community whose names had never been brought to God in prayer. They knew, most certainly, that God did not need anyone's prayers to make Him aware or solicitous of them, but it still seemed right and good to ask a blessing on their behalf. And so they prayed, passing a high-school yearbook around and reading names until all fifteen hundred had been spoken out loud.

Since then, for eighteen years as of this writing, a group of men varying from ten to forty in number has gathered at my house every Thursday morning to continue those prayers, to organize ways of helping people in our community, and to read and discuss the Bible together.

At one of those gatherings, after Gary got sick, someone asked the question: "Do you think we get sadder as we get older? If we are maturing and gaining wisdom as we should, do we at the same time become sadder somehow? Is it okay, maybe even right, to be sad?" We had been reading through a book of the Bible called Ecclesiastes and were looking with particular interest at a verse which says: ". . . with much wisdom comes much sorrow; the more knowledge, the more grief."[11]

The men present were mostly fifty years old and older, the majority over sixty. They were men, black and white, who had lived through considerable historical change. All had seen and suffered from items on the inventory of human imperfection: war, addiction, death, divorce, prejudice, parenting challenges, betrayal, financial loss, sickness.

I don't recall everything that was said in our conversation that morning, but there was a near consensus among the old guard that life, lived honestly, is a saddening journey. The line of reasoning seemed to run thus: How could any healthy, loving soul see the ruination, the suffering, the self-induced hardships of humanity and not be disheartened by them? No one present that morning would have argued with Job's pronouncement that "man born of woman is of few days and full of trouble."[12]

Gary agreed with that assessment. Despite a buoyant humor that characterized his faith and his demeanor, he lived with the ache that every saint carries in his or her bones, the ache of knowing that he was not, we are not, nearly what we should be.

That knowledge, however, did not embitter or poison him.

Like Jesus, but to an obviously lesser degree, Gary was "a man of sorrows, and acquainted with grief."[13] Wherever he traveled, he carried a consciousness that every person he encountered *was* hurting, *had been* hurt, or *would be* hurt. That awareness played a large part in making him so sympathetic and caring toward others. It was why he worked so hard, prayed so constantly, and wanted so deeply for everyone he knew to experience the love of Christ.

All of us, Gary included, have grown up in a culture that embraces personal "freedom" and the attainment of "happiness" as cardinal virtues. I put those terms in quotations because, like most important words that define our pursuits in life—success, fulfillment, health, and goodness—they tend to be purely self-referential. As legitimate and laudable as such goals might be on their own, they are fatally incomplete if not understood in relation to God. Or so Gary would tell you.

The dominant cultural narrative of our day seems pretty simple: "Be free. Get a lot. Be happy. *Carpe diem*. Only this world, this life, this day matters. And if you wish—indeed, maybe it would be best—leave God out of it." Acknowledging sadness, insisting that it have a rightful place at the table of healthy human experience, seems to fly in the face of our short-sighted hedonistic inclinations. There's nothing wrong with freedom—Jesus came to set us free, after all; there's nothing inherently wrong with getting a lot; and there's nothing wrong with being happy, but only if those things are understood in light of Jesus' teachings and only if our pursuit of them is governed by His definition of love.

When freedom leaves us with the feeling that we are still captive to fear and selfishness and anger, when getting lots of stuff leaves us with the feeling that we are still empty, and when happiness leaves us with the feeling that there must be more, what do we do then?

Gary might say, "Be sad about it."

But that's not all he would say. He would tell us that that sadness, that gnawing sense of incompleteness, that yearning, might well be the grace of God drawing our hearts Christward. He would tell us that it is right to be troubled by the violence and poverty we see in the news—God is troubled too; that it is right to hurt for the world's brokenness—God hurts too; that it is right to mourn for the wide gap that exists between what we are as a race and what we could become—God mourns too.

The gospel of Christ gave Gary, and gives all who embrace it, the freedom to know sadness, to sense weariness, to admit homesickness, and to accept a measure of loneliness in life. It gave him permission to be honest about the heaviness within himself and the hellishness of the world around him.

Gary encouraged me to cultivate a healthy respect for the damage that sin has inflicted and is inflicting on the world. He taught me to accept sadness as a temporary part of that damage and to see that my deepest longings can be awakened in this world but not totally fulfilled by it. He reminded me often to set my heart on things above.

Some might find such thinking escapist, defeatist, or pessimistic. Their critique might go something like this: "If one buys into the notion that the world is bad and we are sad and there's nothing we can do about it, and if life is about hanging on until God takes us to heaven, then life here is a waste of time."

To be clear, sad, to Gary, did not mean unuseful.

Sad did not mean defeated.

Sad did not mean ungrateful or ill-tempered.

Sad did not mean unjoyful.

And sad certainly did not mean idle.

Gary saw no contradiction in loving this world but longing, at the same time, for the better world to come.

His belief in heaven is what made him so tirelessly active in doing good in the various places he lived. When he prayed, "Thy kingdom come on earth as it is in heaven," he did not have only a future "new heavens and new earth" in mind. He was thinking of Hamilton and Sarajevo and Pola de Siero and Mazar-e-Sharif.

Charles Haddon Spurgeon, a nineteenth century pastor from England and one of Gary's favorite to read, wrote a short devotional that explained what I'm trying to express:

> Our hope in Christ for the future is the mainspring and the mainstay of our joy here. It will animate our hearts to think often of heaven, for all that we can desire is promised there. Here we are weary and toilworn, but yonder is the land of rest where the sweat of labour shall no more bedew the worker's brow, and fatigue shall be forever banished. To those who are weary and spent, the word 'rest' is full of heaven. We are always in the field of battle; we are

so tempted within, and so molested by foes without, that we have little or no peace; but in heaven we shall enjoy the victory, when the banner shall be waved aloft in triumph and the sword shall be sheathed, and we shall hear our captain say, "Well done, good and faithful servant." We have suffered bereavement after bereavement, but we are going to the land of the immortal where graves are an unknown thing. Here sin is a constant grief to us, but there we shall be perfectly holy, for there shall by no means enter into that kingdom anything which defileth. . . . Oh! is it not joy, that you are not to be in banishment forever, that you are not to dwell eternally in this wilderness, but shall soon inherit Canaan? *Nevertheless* let it never be said of us, that we are dreaming about the future and forgetting the present; let the future sanctify the present to highest uses. Through the Spirit of God, the hope of heaven is the most potent force for the product of virtue; it is a fountain of joyous effort, it is the cornerstone of cheerful holiness. The man who has this hope in him goes about his work with vigor, for the joy of the Lord is his strength.

—*Morning and Evening*, Oct. 2, Morning

The same point is made a bit differently by C. S. Lewis:

Hope . . . means . . . a continual looking forward to the eternal world. . . . It does not mean we are to leave the present world as it is. If you read history you will find that Christians who did most for the present world were just those who thought most of the next. . . . It is since Christians have largely ceased to think of the other world that they have become so ineffective in this. Aim at heaven and you will get earth "thrown in": aim at earth and you will get neither.[14]

Gary got both.

GARY'S UNDERSTANDING OF THIS wise sadness took shape long before the discovery of his tumor. Something I wrote in August 2008 reflects his thinking even then:

I call it "the long ride home," the drive after telling Gary goodbye at the airport whenever he leaves us for extended times away. His departures are always preceded by the uneasy waits at the terminal, the forced and somewhat awkward conversations, the last brief, hesitant prayers, the final hug, and then the quiet drive back to the farm. We fight back tears, or don't, and usually have little to say for the first fifty miles of the ride. I've thought that the experience might be easier by now, since we've had so much practice, but it isn't.

My dear white-haired Mom and I just said goodbye to Gary, who'll return to Afghanistan later tonight.

Some of mine and Gary's travels in the past eight months—pheasant hunting in South Dakota, touring the gardens of Keukenhof, Holland, and hiking in Montana—have deepened our friendship and have been a pleasant mixture of theology, humor, storytelling, sightseeing, and people watching.

Telling him goodbye is a big deal to me.

Yesterday, I asked Gary to share some thoughts, maybe a word of challenge, with the men's group that meets at my house on Thursday mornings. He chose an interesting passage of Scripture for doing so. From Ecclesiastes 7:2 (NIV): "It is better to go to a house of mourning than to go to a house of feasting." The passage, even without Gary's explanation of it, is thought-provoking, even jarring, to the happy-at-all-cost culture in which we live. Those words were especially poignant to us in light of an accident that took the life of a popular sixteen-year-old high school student last weekend. Gary encouraged us to embrace the hurts, big and small, that come in life, telling us that they simply remind us that the world is broken, that we are small, that there is comfort if we look in the Right Place, and that "this ain't home." He reminded us that there is a sadness that is wise, honest, and appropriate if we are seeing the world around us with compassionate eyes. He reminded us that we are called to be servants, and encouraged us to "walk the Way, teach the Truth, and live the Life" that we have learned from Christ. His departure tonight is proof that he practices what he preaches.

So, with his words still in my ears, I accept tonight's long ride home as one more part of the "long ride Home."

THERE IS A PASSAGE in one of the New Testament letters that was especially compelling to Gary, maybe because it was written to an affluent first-century congregation that reminded him of the twenty-first-century American church.

[G]odliness with contentment is great gain. For we brought nothing into the world, and we can take nothing out of it. But if we have food and clothing, we will be content with that. Those who want to get rich fall into temptation and a trap and into many foolish and harmful desires that plunge men into ruin and destruction. For the love of money is a root of all kinds of evil. Some people, eager for money, have wandered from the faith and pierced themselves with many griefs. . . .

Command those who are rich in this present world not to be arrogant nor to put their hope in wealth, which is so uncertain, but to put their hope in God, who richly provides us with everything for our enjoyment. Command them to do good, to be rich in good deeds, and to be generous and willing to share. In this way they will lay up treasure for themselves as a firm foundation for the coming age, so that they may take hold of the life that is truly life.

—1 Timothy 6:6–10, 17–19 NIV

Gary often made reference to one particular phrase from that passage: "life that is truly life." The implication of the phrase, he pointed out, is that there is a life that is *not* truly life, but rather a counterfeit, a pretense, a corruption of what God meant for life to be—a life that places the unsurrendered self at the center of everything. Gary, on the contrary, would say that the gospel, with its restraints, its surrenders, and its emphasis on loving and serving others, is the road by which we find life that is true.

The honesty of the Bible—the honesty that tells us we are lost without God and that life in this world is under the curse of a dark power—is one of the reasons Gary found it so attractive and credible. In a world saturated with advertisers, half truth, and empty promises, the Word of God is refreshingly blunt.

I once heard it said that we don't read the Bible to get a good self-image. We read it instead to get an *accurate* self-image, meaning a clear perception that includes our glory *and* our grime, that recognizes the miracles *and* the messes that we are. Jesus, the prophets, the apostles, and the saints through the ages, instead of trivializing or ignoring the more troubling aspects of our being—the self-righteousness and the sorrows—spoke with clarity about them and, accordingly, treated the wound of the people as though it were serious.[15] It *is* serious. As is the cure.

Another question in that Thursday morning discussion was this: "Who was the saddest man who ever lived?"

Someone put forth the possibility that if wisdom increases our sorrow, as Ecclesiastes says it will, then the wisest man among us would also be the saddest. Which means, of course, that Jesus might have been the saddest man who ever lived. Maybe. The world's misfortunes and sufferings—personal, communal, political, and economic—must have been a constant burden to Him.

But there is a paradox, a mystery, a sweetness to the gospel that is this: Jesus was also the most joyful soul that ever walked the earth. And among the many promises that He gave us is one that says His joy will be made complete in us. Just as grace swallows sin, and immortality swallows mortality, and light conquers darkness, and love conquers evil—eventualities all promised in Scripture—so too does joy ultimately vanquish sorrow.

Weeping may endure for a night, but joy comes in the morning.

—Psalm 30:5 NKJV

There is a song about the Incarnation that makes me think of Gary and those like him (the Incarnation is what we celebrate at Christmas, the event in which God became flesh in the person of Jesus Christ and lived among us):

> He seemed a walking contradiction,
> Perfect joy and perfect sadness,
> His perfect sanity seemed madness,
> In this world where He's a stranger.[16]

It does seem something of a contradiction, doesn't it, that a person can be joyful and sad at the same time? But Jesus, I gather, was one such person, and He calls us to follow Him with the promise that "in this world you will have trouble. But take heart! I have overcome the world."[17]

Gary did not wear sadness on his sleeve. He held it closely, even privately. His joy, on the other hand, was radiant. His was a cheerful countenance. Ask him how or why, and he might have told you:

"Blessed is the one whose transgressions are forgiven, whose sins are covered."[18]

"Blessed are those who mourn, for they will be comforted."[19]

"Blessed are the pure in heart, for they will see God."[20]

YOU MIGHT BE WONDERING why I am writing about this at such length.

Because I know you.

Because I know that you too are sad or have been sad or

will be sad, maybe deeply so. It is an unavoidable part of life. Much of the hurt we endure is self-inflicted. Some is the fault of others. But we all get our share of it. We are typically told to deny it or drown it or numb it with a thousand small diversions. But I hope—and I know Gary would concur—that you'll have the wisdom to listen to your sadness. Accept it for what it says and follow it to the One who can explain it, heal it, redeem it.

It is tragic to be hopeless. But it is perfectly healthy to be sad, at least for a time. It is right to feel lost. But it is madness to shun the Love that leads us home.

Door

GROWING UP AMONG SOUTHERN storytellers, having childhood friends who were often brash and vocal, and working summer jobs with colorfully verbose eccentrics nurtured in me a great fondness for listening to people talk. The simple request, "Tell me about yourself," has led to some of the most pleasant hours of my life.

My adult years—thirteen in law practice, two in Scotland, and over a decade and a half of travel as a singer/songwriter—continue to be filled with interesting people—writers, musicians, artists, educators and students, farmers and entrepreneurs, politicians and pastors. Those most enjoyable, to my taste anyway, are those who possess a healthy sense of curiosity and wonder, a thoughtfulness that takes life seriously and reflectively without being morose or self-important, an unpretentious concern for others, and a confidence that life is more than can be seen with the eye. Sometimes I get to share only minutes or hours with those good souls—drivers, for instance, who've taken me from an airport to a venue, or people with whom I've shared a long meal—while others have been friends for many years. They have shared with me the inestimable gift of thoughtful conversation. They are interest*ing* because they are interest*ed*, it seems, in everything but themselves. They are unforgettable because they are so self-forgetful.

They are, in a word, humble.

C. S. Lewis had this to say about such people:

> Do you imagine that if you meet a really humble man he will be what most people call "humble" nowadays: he will not be the sort of greasy, smarmy person, who is always telling you that, of course, he is nobody. Probably all you will think about him is that he seemed a cheerful, intelligent chap who took a real interest in what *you* said to *him*. If you do dislike him it will be because you feel a little envious of anyone who seems to enjoy life so easily. He will not be thinking about humility; he will not be thinking about himself at all.[21]

Gary was a humble man.

He never met a stranger. That fact made him a joy to travel with, especially overseas. He was not shy or self-conscious around people he didn't know. He had little or no fear of embarrassment. If he was lost, he asked for help. If he was confused, he got answers. And he did it in such a way that endeared him to the freshly-met folk who rendered him assistance. Laughter was frequently part of those interactions, especially when the language barrier was total and hand signals were the only understandable means of communication.

I can imagine those strangers telling their friends, "I met the most cheerful fellow today, an American of all things."

That same gregariousness followed Gary into cancer treatment. For thirty days—Monday through Friday for six weeks—he took radiation at the same hour each morning in Columbus. During that time, he came to know everyone else whose appointments coincided with his: Pat and Jerry, Mr. Carter, Ricky, Willard, Mr. and Mrs. Robertson, the Hood sisters. Into a waiting room that had seen its share of misery, a room often filled with uneasy silence, Gary brought his gentle good nature. He loved the people, and before long, they all knew it. By the time his treatments were completed, they loved him in return.

Those cancer patients and their families were all very much travelers in a foreign land, learning a language that was altogether new and unsettling to them. Their own Afghanistan.

Early on, Gary told us that he considered the John B. Amos Cancer Center not so much a place of healing as a place of serving. His aim there, as it had been in all the places he lived and worked around the world, was to love people, entirely, with attention not just to their temporary physical needs, but also to their fears and sadness, to the eternal and deep longings of their souls.

Almost every day, he showed up at the Amos Center with candy (we usually had to stop on the way to town so that he could purchase his supply).

"Good morning, Mr. Carter, gitcha some vitamins. I got some special ones just for you today. They'll do ya good." And so on.

He called the candy "vitamins" as he walked from person to person, dispensing the dosages. Early on, before he knew the others or they knew him, it was obvious that some were ill at ease with Gary's friendliness and uncomfortable that he seemed light-hearted in such a serious place. But over time you could see everyone soften to him. When he walked in, the faces of patients and staff alike brightened. The fact that he was one of them, one of the sick and suffering, and that his cancer, unlike many of theirs, held little or no promise of cure gave him license to carry on a bit.

But he was not inconsiderate or obnoxiously jovial. He was all too aware of the pain and suffering around him. If someone was weak or having a difficult morning, Gary was soft-spoken and gentle toward that person. How many times during those weeks did I see him lightly pat a shoulder or whisper to one whose face was pale or who was sleep deprived or weary?

I DON'T KNOW WHAT you think of when you hear the word "worship," but there's a good chance it conjures up something somber or brooding. It might bring to mind things mysterious and attainable only by hyper-religious people. In present-day church culture, the word has come to be almost entirely a musical term—as in "worship songs," "worship pastor," "worship time," or "First we worship and then the preacher brings a message." For Gary, the term was not nearly so narrow. The longer he walked with Christ, the deeper his conviction grew that all of life is worship—"the feeling or expression of reverence and adoration" for God.[22]

To Gary, every activity of life, rightly done and understood, fell within the broad category of "worship." Every word and deed, no matter how small or inconsequential, was a chance to bring gladness to the heart of God. Every encounter was a chance to show the love *of God* to others.

Gary's life made worship and holiness and other equally dismissible notions of faith look desirable, enviable, and at least somewhat achievable.

He made the things of God look good.

Gary's perspective on what it meant to serve others was significantly shaped by the importance that Jesus attached to seemingly insignificant objects: cups of water, coins, seeds of grain, hairs of the head, sparrows. They, as much or more than the miraculous or spectacular, struck Gary as the substance from which the Kingdom of God is built. Likewise, small things done kindly and well.

On several occasions, I heard Gary preach from a short passage in the book of Acts, which says that Jesus "went around doing good."[23] Every *word* of the passage, Gary pointed out, has implications for us.

Jesus. Jesus Himself. Not a proxy (though He does have those). The Servant King did not merely tell His followers what to do. He showed them. "I have set you an example that you should do as I have done for you."[24]

Went. Jesus Christ left His home to be able to offer Himself as our sacrifice and to reach us with the love of God. In similar fashion, we should "go." Kindness is active. It does not merely refrain from hurting others. It does positive good. It does not wait. It reaches out. The followers of Christ are sent ones, doing the King's business. Idleness has no place in the Kingdom. Rest, yes; idleness, no. Gary would sometimes ask, "Where are you and I going?"

Around. The love of Christ is expansive, far reaching. It sees opportunity everywhere. Marketplace, soup kitchen, lunchroom, ball field, neighborhood, distant lands—the church goes "around" to make the gospel known in the world.

Doing. Christ did not merely talk about love. He proved it in ways that people could see, most notably at the cross. He showed that love is a not merely "words or speech, but . . . actions and . . . truth."[25] Gary might ask, "What are you and I doing?"

Good. Do as Jesus did. Be "eager to do what is good."[26] To that end, learn Christ. To do good, one has to know good. The Scriptures are constantly contrasting the wise and the foolish, light and darkness, good and evil. One learns to distinguish them, not to be morally superior or judgmental, but so that he or she can follow Jesus authentically.

Gary was a man who *went around doing good.*

We know little of his day-to-day life for the years he was overseas. Even when I asked him about his work abroad, he answered in ways that brought no attention to himself. But I have no doubt that if we could speak to the people with whom he spent time in the various countries where he lived, they would be effusive in their praise of the ways he went around doing good among them.

HARRIS COUNTY, GEORGIA, HAS five very small towns within its borders. Hamilton is the county seat. Total population of the county is thirty-two thousand or so, which works out to around sixty-nine people per square mile (compared to 3,154 per square mile in Atlanta, an hour and a half to the north.)

We have one high school in the county, about four miles west of the farm. It enrolls approximately fifteen hundred students. Off and on for a couple of years, when Gary was home on furlough, he worked at the high school as a substitute teacher. It was a good place to meet new people and to be engaged with the local community. It also provided him opportunities to serve.

During his stint as a sub, Gary was known among the students for his strictness, his likeability (despite the strictness), and his storytelling. He insisted on respect in the classroom and was swift and severe when addressing infractions. He probably recalled from his own days as a high school student how easy it was to run over substitute teachers. He was not going to let that happen to him. Ironically, his strong hand made him a popular fill-in, not only among the faculty, but among the students as well.

Gary had a standard operating procedure for the class sessions over which he presided. He required the students to do whatever lesson the regular teacher had assigned, and then, for the last twenty minutes or so, he would tell them stories from his travels abroad.

Like all good Americans, Gary was aware, at least in vague terms, of the partition between church and state. It was a partition he begrudgingly accepted, but one that he also tested on a regular basis. He was probably safer doing so in a small Southern town than he would have been elsewhere. But, even here in Hamilton, he sometimes got pushback.

He knew he could not proselytize in the classroom. But he had also been told by those in authority that if a student ever asked him a question that called for a "religious" response (for instance, "What is Easter?" or "What is Ramadan?" or "Why do you bow your head before you eat lunch in the cafeteria?"), he was free to answer it honestly.

And so Gary told stories. He told stories knowing that kids would ask questions.

One of the favorites he told was from the time he spent in Peru. He had gone there to live in the jungle with a young family of American missionaries—a married couple and their two small children. Another young family that worked there with them had left temporarily to have a baby.

Gary flew to Lima. From there, he took a small seaplane to the backcountry. Once outside the airspace around the big city, Gary said they flew over no towns or villages for hours. The plane landed in a river. He got out with his backpack, met the family, and was given a thorough tour—five minutes—of the campsite. There was no electricity, no appliances or modern conveniences, and no civilization within even a few hours' reach.

While there, Gary slept in a thatched hut under mosquito netting. He gathered or killed his food every day (monkeys and mangoes), had a pet parakeet, and spent days cutting trails through the thick jungle as part of an effort to reach a primitive tribe believed to be deep in the rain forest. They never made contact with the tribe during the six months that Gary was there.

Gary once told me that, in some ways, he enjoyed Peru more than any other place he served as a missionary. The simplicity of life there was what he found most pleasant. He said the daylight hours dictated when they began and ended their activities. When the sun came up, they went to work. When the sun went down, everything stopped, and they got under their mosquito nets (unless they were going alligator hunting on the river that night). There was no traffic, nothing to spend money on, no billboards or television, no social engagements, no clocks, none of the trappings—bad or good—of city life. It seems the very picture of stimulus deprivation for some of us who've never camped before. But Gary explained that the days were filled with good work, natural beauty, a strong sense of purpose, occasional interaction with an indigenous community up the river, thoughtful conversation with the family he lived with, and ample time during the night to pray and think.

Gary shared all of this background with the students at the high school, and then he would tell them the story of "The Worm."

When he first arrived in the jungle, Gary had been told he should not go into the river without shoes on. Bare feet were susceptible to waterborne parasites that could enter the body and cause serious infection. On one occasion, Gary disregarded the rule and in short order became feverish. His foot began to show signs of infection, and he found it difficult to walk. His leg began to swell. And swell. And swell some more. Gary began to fear gangrene and was in considerable pain. A parasite had entered Gary's foot through a scratch or at one of the nails and was wreaking havoc on his leg.

There were no doctors or clinics around, so Gary asked his teammate Jason to lance his foot at the abscess. They sharpened Gary's knife to a razor edge. They heated the blade until it was white hot. Gary, in true Wild West fashion, put a gag in his mouth to bite down on.

(By this time, every kid in the classroom is leaning forward, slack-jawed and wide-eyed with interest. Gary, I assure you, is telling the story with all the dramatic flare of a Chinese opera singer.)

Jason barely had to touch the skin with the knife blade. The abscess was tight with infection, and when the metal nicked the skin, a veritable eruption occurred. I am certain Gary used brilliantly graphic language—the kind that sixteen-year-old boys would find grossly entertaining—to describe the appearance of the infectious discharge, its flight pattern, and its immense volume. Most notably, Gary would tell them that along with everything else that came out of the wound, a sizable worm shot out of his foot, a worm that had gorged itself on Gary's flesh between the time it had entered and exited his body.

Gary would then tell the kids that after the abscess had been thoroughly drained, Jason wrapped gauze around a stick, doused it in rubbing alcohol, and prodded deep into the wound to clean it out.

The kids, of course, are repulsed and entertained and hugely intrigued, all at the same time. But what happened next was Gary's favorite part of the story.

He would ask, "Y'all have any questions?"

And always, just as he had hoped and planned, a student would raise his or her hand and say, "Mr. Levi, *why* were you there in the first place?"

And the wall of separation between church and state came a'tumblin' down.

EVENTUALLY, GARY GAVE UP substitute teaching—didn't like the discipline part of it, he said—but he continued to go to the high school at seven fifteen each morning. For three or four days a week, he was predictably there for about forty-five minutes.

He was the school's unofficial doorkeeper.

Gary had been given permission by the administration to stand at the back entrance, used by students who either rode buses or parked their cars in the rear parking lot, and greet the kids as they came into the building each morning. He became a fixture, a genial presence at a place that, for many teenagers, can be lonely, frightening, and inhospitable. Many of the young people Gary greeted in the mornings had no idea he was there voluntarily with no official job in the school system.

He took pains to learn the students' names with the help of the high school yearbook, which he bought every year for that purpose. He tried to know something, however small, of their interests and personalities, and he made extra effort to learn the names of those who seemed least excited to see him each morning. I think he took special pleasure in wearing them down and winning them over. Hundreds of times every morning, he spoke words of greeting and called out a host of first names—Brandon, Crystal, Monterio, Alexis, Kwan, Britney, Catravious, Zach, Trey. He made the back door of the high school more than just an entry point.

For the students, it became a place of welcome.

For Gary, it was a place of worship.

Over the course of the school year, often through short conversations at the back door, Gary learned of needs in the lives of individual students and their families. And then, as anonymously as he could, he made gifts or took steps to ensure they were cared for.

On Valentine's Day, he would send or give flowers to girls—the not so popular ones—that he thought might be overlooked on that special day.

Upon learning of one disabled student who lived in a housing project with his single mom and who liked to fish but never had the chance to go, Gary took him.

At each year's end, he chose four or five students and with permission of their parents and the school administration, took them out of class for a day trip to Atlanta. These were excursions of pure fun—a fancy meal at a restaurant over-looking the city, a visit to a tourist attraction or a place of local interest, and a big dessert on the way home. All out of his own generous pocket.

Gary was always on the prowl for ways to bless the students. Which brings Reggie to mind.

This is what I wrote on the day it happened:

Sunday, March 25, 2007

As I write this, I'm at a Starbucks in Augusta, Georgia, en route from last night's gig in Sumter, South Carolina, to tonight's in Athens, Georgia. It is 12:15, midday, and in a short while, a couple hundred miles from here, the NASCAR race in Bristol, Tennessee, will begin. It's been on my mind all morning, not just because I've become a racing fan, but because . . . well, let me just tell you the story.

At the Harris County High School, where Gary and I spend time as Young Life volunteers, there is a beloved student in the special needs class named Reggie. He is an enthusiastic, friendly, helpful, lovable young man who has a passion for NASCAR, driver Jeff Gordon in particular. His mom told us that Reggie did not speak much until he was three years old. It was then that he saw a NASCAR race on television and instantly developed a fascination for the sport. Seems that all of those speeding automobiles woke up something in Reggie. He has followed stock car racing avidly, and I do mean avidly, ever since.

While Reggie has a difficult time with many of the classes at the high school, he has a steel-trap memory for the facts and figures of NASCAR. Want to know the angle of turn three at any racetrack in America, or who won third in points back in 2003, or who drives the 27 car, or who is crew chief for any of the teams? Just ask Reggie.

My brother met Reggie a couple of years ago when Reggie was an underclassman. Now that Reggie is a senior, just a couple of months from graduation, Gary wanted to do something special for him. When Gary decides to do something special for someone, I make sure I'm in a position to take notes and to catch the joy that spills out of the cup of his intended beneficiary.

I have a friend whom I met through Young Life years ago. She is a well-connected member of the NASCAR organization and, more importantly, loves Christ and loves kids. When Gary asked for her phone number, having in mind to ask for tickets to a race, I offered him little encouragement. I didn't have much hope that Kathy, an extremely busy person during race season, would be able to make time for him. (You do know about the popularity of NASCAR and the scarcity of tickets, don't you? Especially at races like Daytona and Bristol?) Gary, undaunted and against the odds, called her anyway to make a bold request: "Is it possible to get a couple of tickets to a race, any race, and—*gulp*—maybe get Reggie a pit pass?" A pit pass would allow him to walk through the garage area, around the cars and drivers, before the race began.

One of the most coveted tickets in NASCAR is the one to Bristol Motor Speedway. The venue seats 160,000 people who look over a track that is less than half a mile long. When Kathy, just two weeks ago, told Gary that she *would* send him two tickets to that race, with pit passes, he cried. When he told Reggie's mom, she cried. When Reggie found out he'd be going to the race, he immediately packed his suitcase for the longest trip he's ever taken away from home.

Yesterday, Gary and Reggie drove to Asheville, North Carolina, their stopping point for the night. They woke up at 4:30 this morning to complete the drive to Bristol.

Just minutes ago, I spoke with them. Their gladness and excitement leapt through the phone line. Already today, thanks to Kathy, Reggie has taken a ride around the Bristol track in the pace car (a *very* rare privilege), courtesy of driver Jeff Bodine. He has met a number of drivers and crew chiefs. He has been in the pits all morning around people he has watched on television for the past fourteen years. He has walked on the track, which to this point has been known to him only in pictures and statistics. He has been given hats, shirts, and, best of all, a lug nut off the 24 car, driven by Jeff Gordon.

Might it be that when I met Kathy and her family years ago, God was setting in place a gift for Reggie? Might it be that when Kathy began her career that put her in a place of influence with NASCAR, He was giving, in addition to an income and vocation for her and her family, a gift for Reggie? Might it be that when Gary met Reggie as a substitute teacher at the high school, God was planning this very day? Might all these small dots have been placed on the map of history for this moment, this beautiful Sunday afternoon? This is what the choreography of coinci-dance looks like.

In the grand mystery of cause and effect, might all those things have happened for the sake of a pit pass, some handshakes, a wish-made-good, a dream come true?

The God revealed in Scripture is a God of grand things—of light years and lunar eclipses, of

landscapes and longitudes, of quasars and earth-
quakes. On this day, at this hour, He is all that, but
He is also Lord of loud cars and lug nuts.

When Gary got sick, Reggie's mom brought him to the
farm for a visit. Reggie told Gary how much he loved him,
expressed how Gary had been like a father to him, and remembered how Gary had given him the best day of his life.

Months later, at Gary's funeral, Reggie was a pallbearer,
one young face representing a throng of others who attest to
the kindness of Mr. Levi.

GARY ENJOYED BEING AT the high school in the morning, but
he also had a purpose for being there. It was his prayer—I
know because I often heard him pray it—that through so
small a gesture, students would encounter and be drawn, in
some way beyond his telling, to the person, the love, and the
truth of Christ.

To be clear, Gary did not believe that human kindness could
save a soul, neither the soul being kind nor the soul receiving the
kindness. It might help, but it could not complete the work. No
accomplishment or virtue—morality, philanthropy, humanitar-
ianism, patriotism, political affiliation, activism, nor any other
goodness—could put someone in right standing with God. The
person of Jesus—His birth, life, death, and resurrection—is
alone able to complete that work. And Gary was emphatic that
the propositional truth of the Gospel *had to be* communicated by

spoken or written means so that people could hear it, believe it, and live it out as an act of the will and intellect.

So, why kindness? It was Gary's hope that deeds done in the spirit of Christ and with the love of Christ might crack a heart open and draw someone toward the sweetness of the gospel.

I can imagine someone thinking this all sounds manipulative and insincere. Like it's all some kind of *pretend* kindness. Quite the contrary. Believing as he did that God is kind, Gary felt duty bound—happily so—to cultivate that same attribute in himself, regardless of whether others responded to it or not. And he prayed that just as God's kindness leads people to Christ and repentance, his would do likewise. But if it didn't, he would be kind just the same, for the sheer goodness of it.

So Gary stood at the door—not as a "random act of kindness," but purposefully—hoping that those children would someday know the love of Christ for their own. He stood at the door not as a *have to* but as a *get to*.

When Gary became sick and his days at the back door were winding down (because it was hard for him to stand, hard to remember names, difficult to wake so early), the high school students, with support from the administration, planned an assembly to thank and honor him. The event—which began with hundreds of kids rising to their feet and applauding his entrance—was a complete surprise to Gary. When he walked into the crowded room and it dawned on him what was taking place, he bowed his head and cried. To the adult friends and family in attendance, the event was an affirmation that Gary's commitment to do small things kindly and well over a long period of time had not been in vain.

Even before we learned of Gary's cancer, I had been working on a short song for him called "Doorkeeper's Prayer." I finished it, a bit too hurriedly perhaps, so that Gary could record it soon after he got sick. He had never heard it before, had no time to learn it, and was tired when we went to the studio late one afternoon. Good sport that he was, he sang through it for me.

The lyric alludes to a passage of Scripture from the Psalms that speaks of being a doorkeeper in the temple of the Lord.[27] I think the words imperfectly but accurately reflect what was in Gary's heart and mind when he went to the high school each morning.

Let my presence be a prayer,
To every soul that enters here,
Let each welcome that I share,
Be the voice of God.

Let this gesture, very small,
Bless each kid who walks these halls,
Let them sense the calling of
The great and gracious God.

Some see just a simple door,
Glass and steel and nothing more,

But here I worship Christ, the Lord,
Of ocean, earth, and sky.

Gladly do I serve You here,
Daily bring my offering,
I, a keeper of Your door,
In the castle of the King,

With the love of Christ the King.

SPEAKING OF DOORS, GARY had two to his house: a front and a back. One led to his garage and workshop, the other to his front porch.

There were two small handwritten notes taped to each of the doors. By the time he passed away, the writing on them had begun to fade.

One, on a yellow Post-it note, read:

Only one life,
'Twill soon be past,
Only what's done
For *Christ* will *last*.

The other contained a question and answer:

Is today the day I die?
Live it well.

My guess is that Gary put them there so that each time he left his house, he would do so with intention—to live for what matters most. Those words on the door were his map, his marching orders, his compass. They were sobering reminders that even at his strongest moments, his life—all our lives— hung by a thread. Live for what matters most.

Heaven

SOME PEOPLE SCOFF AT the notion of heaven. Rightly so perhaps. If one makes it trivial enough—harps all day, baby bottoms, Hallmark cards, clouds—it does come off as a laughable construct. Same as hell.

If heaven is a reality, though, and if Christ is the architect and builder of it, then it stands to reason that such a place would reflect His character, that it would be an outward expression of Him, just as other parts of creation are—everything from a flower petal to sexual pleasure to northern lights. Right thinking about heaven requires more work, more imagination, and more humility than most of us are willing to invest in the subject. I've met few who give it very much time or energy. But Gary did. Joyfully so.

Even those who deny or belittle the notion of everlasting life probably think about it when faced with their own death or that of a loved one. Sanity dictates that we do so. There are reasonable questions to ask even if one concludes that they are ultimately unanswerable. Do we live on? Do we have immortal souls? What happens to our bodies at death? Is there heaven? Is there hell? Is there nothing?

Long before Gary got sick, he spoke frequently about death—about death in general and about his own in particular. ("Is this the day I die? Let me live it well.") He spoke of it with appropriate seriousness, but he also spoke of it longingly. That is not to imply anything pathological or morbid. It is simply to recognize Gary's belief that the gospel, to paraphrase George Herbert, had transformed death from an executioner into a gardener.

If there is a God—a good, caring, loving God (and I realize that is a very big "if" to many people)—it is unthinkable that such a God would remain silent and leave us enslaved to fear about the only event we can be certain of in life. Gary was persuaded that Jesus—that good, caring, loving God in the flesh—had spoken clearly and hopefully to the subject of human mortality. Two phrases, one spoken *by* Jesus and the other *about* Him, stand out in particular—"It is finished" and "He (Christ Himself) is risen."

WHEN GARY GOT SICK, especially early on, his thoughts and comments gravitated to a phrase, "better by far," that had been written by the Apostle Paul to one of the first-century churches. The phrase comes from this passage:

For to me, to live is Christ and to die is gain. If I am to go on living in the body, this will mean fruitful labor for me. Yet what shall I choose? I do not know! I am torn between the two: I desire to depart and be with Christ, which is better by far; but it is more necessary for you that I remain in the body.

—Philippians 1:21–24 NIV

I've never known anyone who looked forward to heaven more than Gary did. And his anticipation was not because he lived a dire, dread existence here, not because he wanted to escape from some horrible pain or poverty. Gary thrived and lived life to the full in this world, but he really did believe that heaven was his home. The last passage of Scripture he memorized was 2 Corinthians 4:16–18 (NIV). I still have in my Bible the creased piece of notebook paper he carried in his pocket to help him commit those words to his fading memory.

[W]e do not lose heart. Though outwardly we are wasting away, yet inwardly we are being renewed day by day. For our light and momentary troubles are achieving for us an eternal glory that far outweighs them all. So we fix our eyes not on what is seen, but on what is unseen, since what is seen is temporary, but what is unseen is eternal.

From the time he learned of his illness, Gary was emphatic: "Death, as frightening as it might be, is not the worst thing that can happen to me." I consistently heard him ask people not just to pray for his healing (which they all seemed keen to do), but also to ask for God's best, which might *not* be healing. If he were to get well, and if he were able to serve Christ for years to come in this world, fine and good. But Gary was comfortable with the alternative. He had told all his doctors, in his first meetings with each of them, that he wanted them to tell him the unvarnished truth concerning his condition and possible treatments. And I think he startled a couple of them when he told them, concerning treatment possibilities, that "death is not a bad option." At least one of the doctors seemed irritated by that pronouncement, but I think he knew Gary was not simply playing brave.

I believe that Gary endured his six-week round of radiation and chemotherapy as a kindness to the family. He had left decisions concerning treatment up to us, given the cloudiness of his own thinking. Brain cancer in 2011 was difficult to treat with any significant hope of long-term success (perhaps that will have changed by the time you read these pages). We were informed from the start that the likely results of treatment were not promising. Still, we felt that the risk of one cycle of radiation and chemo was small and opted to pursue that course.

We were told anecdotally that one patient, an elderly man in his nineties, had been treated for a glioblastoma just like Gary's, had gone into remission, and had just gotten married!

Gary was impressed but also chuckled, saying that "they kept the old guy alive but clearly destroyed his ability to make decisions."

I'm thankful that Gary took treatments. The time he spent at the Amos Cancer Center gave him a healthy sense of purpose, and I'm confident that others benefited from his presence there. It also gave us as a family the opportunity to meet Dr. Pippas, Dr. Ciuba, and Cindy Ivey, all of whom gave (and continue to give) a compassionate face to the practice of oncological medicine.

But most importantly, I'm convinced that the treatments gave us additional months to be with Gary.

"Death is not a bad option."

Gary could be so bothersome at times.

And so right.

THOUGH GARY'S FAITH REMAINED strong throughout the cancer season, he was not without his moments of questioning. The process of dying slowly, of losing strength and faculties and dignity a little at a time, was degrading and humiliating. Gary was not immune from the embarrassment that came with his illness. He rarely complained, but I can recall one conversation at the end of a particularly difficult day in which he expressed his very honest confusion—and disappoint-ment—about the apparent pointlessness of it all. "I just can't understand why God would make us go through this. If I had a child, I don't think I would make them suffer like this. I can't see the good in this." It was the only time Gary voiced his doubt to me. I didn't have the heart to suggest that God might be letting Gary linger so that we, the family, might have a little more time with him.

LET ME SAY SOMETHING here for sake of clarity.

Gary's perspective on death—its desirability, its better by far-ness, its inevitability—might make it sound as if he believed, or that Christians believe, that death is a good thing.

Please hear me: Death is not a good thing. It is a terrible, hideous, unnatural intrusion into God's creation. It is not a good thing.

Likewise, suffering is not a good thing. Loss is not a good thing. Sickness is not a good thing.

And Gary, in longing to be with Christ, would never have said that any of those are good in themselves. He would be quick to point out that suffering and dying only exist in human experience because of sin's presence in the world. And if we didn't already know, he would explain its entrance into the world by teaching us of "The Fall," that Adam-and-Eve event that took us away from God in the Garden of Eden.

One of the glories of the gospel, however, and Gary knew this well, was that "in all things God *works for the good* of those who love Him."[28] All things are not good. But all things are subservient to the transformative power of God. And the worst parts of human history and individual loss can be used to bring about the healing purposes of God, so that "suffering produces perseverance; perseverance, character; and character, hope."[29] Even death, the trespasser in the Garden, has been transformed into the key that opens the gate of our return.

Am I clear? Death is an awful, hideous thing. But thankfully, it is a defeated thing that betrays itself every time it tries to take a child of God.

THE OCCASION OF GARY'S death has caused me to think much about heaven. I have wondered, for instance, where Gary *is* right now? In what state of being does he exist? Is he sleeping? Is he sentient? Is he conscious of the land he left behind?

I've wished at times that the Bible provided more information about heaven. But maybe that would be too distracting for some of us. Perhaps it would make us suicidal in an overeagerness to get there? For now, at least to my reading of it, the Bible gives only the vaguest hints as to what's next. The fact that Jesus spoke of heaven at all—with assertions of eternal life, with the fact of His own resurrection to assure its reality, with the promise of His return, and with His own ascension to a *place*—was more than enough to bolster Gary's faith in its existence, whether he knew the particulars of it or not.

To those who are certain of the whereabouts and the activities of the departed, I can only say "maybe" to most of what they assert. Maybe it is that way.

Might it be, however, that God doesn't want my focus to be on heaven, but to be on Him? Not on the "kingdom come" but on the kingdom now? Not on what is being prepared but on what is presently before us? "Just learn who I am and how I love you," God seems to be saying to me these days, "and you'll be fully at ease trusting Me with what is yet to come."

That said, nothing in Scripture seems to forbid the Christian from imagining the place to which he or she is bound, or from considering what a painless, unhurried, stressless, peaceful, undying world might be like. *Better by far.*

Would Gary have been thankful for healing? I think so. We, his family, would have been over the moon with gratitude. But we knew from the start what we were up against. And we who were closest to him were as amazed as anyone by the perspective—so different from our own—that Gary brought to his end of life. That perspective was set forth candidly in an email he sent to friends on the day following his diagnosis:

> *"Bless the Lord, O my soul, and all that is within me bless His holy name."*

> I don't know where to begin in expressing my gratitude for all the calls, notes, emails, Skype calls, and Facebook messages I have received in the past couple of days. I was hoping to answer each of you individually but now see that that might not be possible given the present circumstances. I am assuming that most of you now know that I have been diagnosed with a malignant tumor on the left side of my brain.

Many of you are praying for my healing. Thank you. I am praying for His will, that He will use this for His glory and honor, and that He will draw us all closer to Himself. Selfishly, a part of me is praying to go home. Like yourself, perhaps, I am tired of the struggles in this life, the fight with self and the flesh. Every day it seems I am more and more aware of my need and my weakness. I long to see Christ face to face, with a glorified mind, soul, and body and to be as He is. I'm not sure what will happen, but I know the One who does, and I rejoice in the fact that He rejoices in doing me good.

It may seem strange, but I am excited about the possibility of going home soon. My brother wrote a song with the title, "The First of Us to Go." We both long to go to our eternal home. I have often felt as Paul did when he wrote that he longed to depart and be with Christ, which is better by far. While I struggle with the thought of leaving loved ones that are dear to my heart, I hope that in each one of us there is a longing to be with Christ, a longing for home, a longing to be with the One who loves us more than we can imagine, and a desire to be in that place where we will be able to love Him back perfectly.

Life has been good to me in this fallen world, largely because of ones like you, but I know that there is something better, and I want to fall asleep and wake up there. What a task and blessing I have now of thanking all of you who have enriched my life by allowing me to see Christ more clearly through your walk. Let's continue to press on and obey Him until He returns. Your life enriches mine, and I am blessed by our paths having crossed. My life and times, like yours, are in His hands. If He chooses to keep me here, I pray that I will love Him more and more, fight for His honor, glory, and kingdom. And if He chooses to take me home, I will praise Him until you arrive.

I love you with the bonds of Christ.

Gary

In letters that Gary wrote to friends and family over the years, it was not unusual for him to conclude with a curious phrase—"perhaps today."

The two words were intended as a sobering but not unhappy statement about the fleeting and fragile nature of our lives. Gary meant by them to remind us that at any moment, perhaps today, we might take our final breath in this world. They were offered as an honest encouragement to live wisely. They were an expression of hope and a promise of heaven. They were a looking forward to that time when we would be free from every form of suffering and from every hurt, regret, and fear that we carry through life because we are sinners.

But the phrase was also one of warning, intended to make us ask uncomfortable questions: "Am I ready for death should it come to me this very day? Have I made peace with the fact that at some point in time my heart will stop beating, my body will be laid to rest, and, if Jesus' words are true, I will have to give account for my life, to spend eternity with or apart from Him?"

At Gary's memorial service, these words were printed in the program: "We gather today to celebrate, even as we grieve the loss of his presence, that, for Gary, there is no more 'perhaps.' The everlasting and joyful day is now his. He has crossed over. He is home."

Shortcomings

IF THIS WERE AN attempt to reconstruct Gary's life in detail, I suppose I'd be obligated to devote appropriate space to describing his shortcomings. A very short chapter would suffice. I don't think I would find very much to say. That might merely indicate a lack of objectivity on my part, but then it might just be the truth.

In an effort, however, to paint a full-bodied portrait of my brother, here are some things you'd have seen if you'd spent time with him:

He had a bad habit of interrupting people when they were speaking, especially if he disagreed with what they were saying. If they didn't yield the floor, he would just talk over them. He was aware of this impolite tendency but made little progress against it.

He refused to spend money on new clothes.

He mispronounced certain words every time he used them,

especially when reading out loud. "Deaf" was always "death," "hellion" was always "helliard," and "therefore" was always "thereforth."

He could be intolerant of viewpoints that he believed offensive to the gospel. I'm not sure he saw anything wrong with that, so long as he was civil and gracious toward those holding the offending point of view. He felt a duty to respect the *rights* of people to hold whatever views they wanted, but he did not feel any duty to respect the view itself.

The same curiosity that made him so eager to learn, see, and try new things made it difficult for him to stick with one interest for very long—the gospel being the one notable exception to that.

He could, in the eyes of some at least, be overly serious at times. For instance, he was quick to walk out of movies that were off-color or used the name of Christ profanely (in other words, many of the movies he went to).

Abuse of political power, government waste, and hypocrisy in leadership—all of which he saw in generous portions everywhere he lived—bothered him greatly.

He rarely washed his hands before he ate.

To Gary's credit, if others criticized him or if he realized he had acted unkindly toward someone—usually because of something he said or the manner in which he said it—he was quick to admit fault, happy to ask forgiveness, and eager to make amends. He was mindful of God's ongoing work in his life. The small failures were daily reminders of why he had come to Christ in the first place.

There you have it. He was a fallen, failed, in-need-of-forgiveness member of the human race. A "messed up mixture of glory and grime."[30]

Book

WHEN I CANCELLED ALL of my travels to stay home and care for Gary, I assumed I would have considerable time for reading—not an unpleasant prospect.

Gary took naps every day after lunch. I tried to spend that time reading in the quiet room where he slept, but was usually too tired to do so. Looking back now, I probably read less in the cancer year than I have in the past three decades.

Gary and I have been enthusiastic readers for most of our adult lives. Neither of us had televisions. Most of our news was from the radio, usually NPR. Much of our leisure time over the years has been spent with books.

I don't know that reading was ever easy for Gary, but he was convinced that without books his understanding of the gospel would always be malnourished. He read Scripture devotedly and systematically. He made it a practice to read the Bible at least twice a year, cover to cover. Biographies of missionaries, sermons (especially those of C. H. Spurgeon), devotional works, and history were also parts of his regular reading diet.

You have probably gathered by now that Gary was thoroughly biblical in his orientation to life. He had a profound reverence for Scripture, understood the world according to what it taught, predicated his moral and ethical judgments on its teachings, and believed its dogma to be essential to a right relationship with God. He was not uncritical in his reading of the Bible, however, and was quick to acknowledge its complexities. But that did not shake his confidence in its reliability nor undermine its authority as his rule for faith and practice.

I know that, probably even in my family, there are many perspectives concerning what the Bible is. To some it is pure fiction. To others it's a compilation of mythical moral suggestions. Some consider it loosely but unreliably historical. Some see it as the way to God. Others consider it diabolical for the cruelty it has sanctioned in the world. For some it is the message of true freedom. Others say it is a weapon of oppression. To some it is intellectually inexhaustible. To others it is the brain food of idiots, irrelevant to twenty-first-century life. Some deem it timeless and true in a way that no other writing will ever be. Some deem it the flawed work of uninspired human hands. Others call it the Word of God.

Gary appreciated that people had different perspectives and beliefs concerning the Bible. He was charitable toward those who had honest questions and uncertainties about what it says and means. But he had little patience with those who were openly disrespectful or contemptuously irreverent of Scripture. Gary's suspicion was that among the Bible's detractors, its teachings "[had] not been tried and found wanting; it [had] been found difficult and left untried."[31] And he felt that, if only for the far-reaching influence it has had on the world for the better, the Bible was entitled to the courtesy of its critics. At a minimum, neighborliness and good manners, if nothing else, dictated that people be respectful of a book that was honored by so many.

Here again, Gary practiced what he preached. He was familiar with, though certainly no student of, the sacred texts of world religions. If he disavowed them, he tried to do so graciously, out of respect for the fact that to others those books were venerable.

To Gary, the Scriptures, taken together, told a story—*The Story*—of the world.

It was *his* story. It is *my* story. If you don't mind my saying so, it is *yours* too. The plot rambles. The characters confound. The language befuddles. The narrative voice shifts. The words are at times crystal clear and at others ambiguous and seemingly contradictory. But it *is* our story, or God's story about us, whether we want it to be or not.

I can assure you that the Bible was *the* book that prepared me for and carried me through the cancer season. It reminded me often that death is not a wall but a door, not a conclusion but a graduation.

GARY WOULD ENCOURAGE YOU to read good, or better yet, *great* books. What a gift they were to him. Could Jim Elliot as he kept his journals, or J. C. Ryle when he wrote his essays, or C. S. Lewis when he penned his writings possibly have imagined the deep and far-reaching effects that their printed words would have on the lives of those like Gary?

I hope you have books like the ones he treasured, ones that stir your heart and deepen your appreciation for life. While words may have many and obvious limitations, their mastery and careful use do much to shape our thoughts and give clarity to our experiences. They did that in Gary's life, on everything from how to call a turkey to why one should fast and pray.

Lest I've painted a too-narrow impression of his reading habits, let me mention that Gary also enjoyed reading fiction and history. He rarely went anywhere without a book to read in case he had a few minutes of free time.

ONE ASIDE:

I don't recall many of the books that I read during the year of that long goodbye, but one does stand out: *The Adventures of Tom Sawyer.*

In such a heavy season of life, it was nice to have a healthy distraction from the burden of constant vigil. The colorful world of Tom Sawyer was one such distraction for me. I've been an avid fan and reader of Mark Twain since childhood.

In high school, I stole a number of Twain books from the school library. It didn't look to me like anyone was making use of them, and I thought Mr. Twain might appreciate that I had risked criminal prosecution to own his writings. My moral compass was in a bad magnetic field at the time. Decades later, I returned all of those books to the high school and offered to pay the hefty fine I owed. The librarian was generous in her forgiveness, and we negotiated a suitable settlement.

I now own a shelf full of Twain's writings. All paid for.

People gave or recommended any number of books to me after Gary got sick. Most of them were deeply ponderous or theological in nature. They were offered, I am sure, with the best of intentions, but I don't think I finished any of them.

I did, however, finish *Tom Sawyer* and was sad to see it come to an end. Interesting that the story of a long-ago boy in a world full of adventure, wit, and superstition—a story written by a man who, because of so much death in his own family, had a difficult time accepting the notion of a benevolent God—would be the one text that I most remember from the cancer season.

Perhaps there's a bit of Tom in Gary's story.

WHEN YOU COME TO my house, you might notice a framed shadowbox on the credenza as you enter the front door. In the shadowbox is a small gray book that belonged to Gary. The faded title on the cover, the smudges on the pages, the frayed edges of the binding, the barely-legible lists of names that it contains, all bear witness to its frequent use.

Of all the earthly possessions that Gary left behind, this was the one I most wanted for myself.

It was his prayer book, in which he wrote the names of people he wanted to remember when he spent time alone with God.

My name is written in that book.

Every family member's name is written in it.

Hundreds of names are there—friends, neighbors, acquaintances, colleagues, others. Some I knew; many I don't.

The book contains some printed text, mostly psalms and other Scripture, but Gary valued it primarily for the names he'd written in it.

I don't know how long Gary had used that particular prayer book, but I have a picture, from the morning of Christmas Eve 1990, in which he is holding it. The photo was taken in Cerler, a very small town in northern Spain near the French border—the highest village in the Aragon Pyrenees. It was Gary's suggestion that we go there for Christmas that year.

I was living in Scotland at the time, and Gary was living in Madrid. I flew to Spain. We spent several days in Madrid and then drove 330 miles from southwest to northeast, stopping whenever we felt like doing so, hiking along the way, eating leisurely meals, sharing stories, and comparing notes about life in Europe.

It might well be the most memorable Christmas of my life.

On the overcast afternoon of December 25, we took a long walk through the snow, into the hills outside the village. We served communion to one another with wine and bread we'd purchased from a small grocer. At the hillside where we had communion, we took some photographs and recorded a message on cassette tape that we mailed to Mom and Dad.

It was a day blessedly quiet and slow. It was a bachelor's Christmas, not better than one full of children and gifts and holiday sounds, but different in a welcome way.

THE COVER OF GARY'S prayer book has been worn bare where his fingers rested. He tended to hold it with both hands, thumbs on the inside to keep it open.

I can only imagine how many times, and in how many places, for how many hours altogether, Gary had that little book in his grip. Its passport, if it had had one, would be impressive.

Whenever he was home, I could look across the pasture early in the morning—he and I typically awoke before sunrise—and see his reading light on. I could be sure he was sitting in the chair beside his fireplace, drinking the strong coffee he enjoyed so much, and spending his time quietly as he began the day. A Bible and the little gray prayer book would be close at hand.

The benefit of that book to him, when he was far from home, was that it allowed him to keep his family and friends nearby. It was a token that helped him remember and carry the neighborhood with him wherever he went.

The benefit to us for whom he prayed can never be known, at least not in this world.

Eunice Bearden, my grandmother on my mother's side, was an old-school country woman—try to picture something along the lines of Grant Wood's "American Gothic"—who worked hard, lived poor (or very close to it), and was a product of rural Mississippi. She had a meager education and could boast little in the way of credentials or accomplishment, aside from five children and a long list of survival skills.

When Gary and I were college students, Mama Bearden used to send us religious books once or twice a year. They were usually written by an early-era televangelist who always seemed a bit dubious to me. Still does. I never read any of the books but was glad to receive them because they always came with cash, usually small denominations. The books were evidence of Mama Bearden's hope that I might become a man of faith someday.

When I ponder, as I sometimes do, why I became a Christian, I think of her. Specifically, I think of her prayers. And I wonder what role those simple, unpolished pleas might have played in the long chain of cause and effect that lead to my salvation. Perhaps they were why at the end of my undergraduate years, I began to follow Christ, and why, a year or so later, Gary would do likewise.

As news of Gary's illness became known, we received a steady flow of notes, emails, cards, and calls. They came from all manner of folk—some as rustic as Mama Bearden, others the very picture of refinement—and from all manner of places around the world. They represented a wide range of wealth, power, and education. They all assured us that they were offering prayers for Gary. We trusted that God, no respecter of persons, would hear them all and answer rightly.

But we also trusted this: that God—mystery of mysteries—was praying *with* us. To the prayers of ones like Eunice and

Reggie and Jolley and Walker were added those of the godhead, according to a promise:

> [T]he Spirit helps us in our weakness. For we do not know what to pray for as we ought, but the Spirit himself intercedes for us with groanings too deep for words.
>
> —Romans 8:26 ESV

Prayer has been, and continues to be, a curious and inexplicable part of faith for me. I know it is essential to the Christian life. It is a duty, but I have heard some say that it is also a delight. I confess that I pray in large part because I'm supposed to. But I also confess that sometimes there are moments of splendor and deep peace—moments full of promise—when I open my heart to God.

I think Gary took real delight in prayer, and he was genuinely grieved when, after getting sick, he told us, "I can't pray anymore. My mind won't let me."

I know Gary's prayer book is only paper and ink, insubstantial on its own and destined to go the way of all things temporal. But there is a sacredness about it. In some ways, it was where he loved me—us—best of all. It was the physical place, like an altar he kept in his suitcase, where he met with Christ each day. None, or very few of us, ever saw the small sacrifices he made for us during his quiet hours of intercession. There were no congratulations or profit to him for taking our names into the presence of God. There was no assurance that he would ever see any visible result from his prayers.

But pray he did. The book is proof that he did so devotedly. It is a framed reminder of how much he loved God and how much he loved people.

It's one more small but telling thing.

Hope

ON CHRISTMAS DAY 2011, Gary's last with us, I shared the following message with friends:

> Some years ago, shortly after I left law practice to try my hand as a full-time singer/songwriter, I had a conversation with an old friend, a thoroughly modern man from Atlanta, who understood the business of music. He was very encouraging, spoke favorably of my meager musical and lyrical abilities, and gave me reason to believe that, from purely economic angles, I could survive as a musician. (While mildly curious about things Christian, he was not a man of faith.) His one concern, a sizable one, was that the songs I was writing were not edgy or raw enough, and that the view of life described in them was hardly recognizable to jaded

twentieth-century listeners. His advice was that I darken things up a bit so that they feel more like the actual world. My songs, he said, were out of touch with reality and naively optimistic.

In short, they contained too much hope, a charge to which I plead guilty.

Last week in a reading from the Old Testament, I came across an interesting phrase that brought to mind my conversation with that thoroughly modern man. Zechariah the prophet is speaking to Israel, the favored people of God who, for decades, had been living as slaves far away from their native land. They are finally going home when God, speaking through the prophet, tells them:

"Return to your fortress, you *prisoners of hope.*"[32]

Prisoners of hope, he calls them.

Is hope a prison?

Regret, delusion, greed, bitterness, addiction—I can easily see how we get locked inside those walls. But hope?

I've pondered those words today, especially in light of the past five months, and they're starting to make sense to me as I realize my place among the gratefully incarcerated.

I am a prisoner.

I am bound by hope.

Because of Christmas.

One could argue that to believe in the Christmas story—to be convinced that God loved this broken world and gave Himself to it by pouring Himself into the thimble of a human body in order to bring the whole ruined lot of us back to paradise—is to be captive to a calm certainty that goodness is at work and, cliché though it might sound, everything is going to be okay.

Christmas takes us prisoner, makes us inescapably people of faith and hope and love.

And knowing that to be true, the angel can sing now, as he did then, "Behold, I bring you good tidings of great joy."

Gary continues to live and inspire us with *his* hope, even as he deals with increasing weakness and fatigue. We've had the recent gift of good days that included short walks outside, visits with friends, foodfoodfood, and freedom from discomfort. We laugh just as we have before, even if we are quite tired at times.

Merry Christmas, you dear friends. Your kindnesses continue to be daily reminders of Emmanuel, "God with us."

Thank you,
—allen

Unheroic

"NEVER MARRIED," AS I'VE already hinted, was a status Gary gladly accepted. While it was not without challenges, he did not consider it to be a burden or curse that God had visited upon him.

When asked or teased about being a bachelor, Gary would sometimes reply, with a mixture of humor *and* earnestness, that he *was* married—married to Christ. And in the same way that a married person has an obligation to love, to serve, to honor, to submit, and to remain faithful to his or her spouse, so Gary felt those obligations to his Lord.

He recognized that singleness wrongly understood could lead to a life of pointless self-absorption. Unmarried people without children who sense no responsibility to others, and who have only their desires, appetites, and opinions to guide them can fall prey to the idea that they are free to do whatever they wish with whatever they have. They are lords of small kingdoms. Gary functioned out of a very basic principle taken from the plain reading of Scripture: He was *not his own*, he had been bought with a price, and he was obliged to honor Christ with everything he had—his time, his money, his body, his aspirations. He saw himself as a steward, a trustee, or as he sometimes wrote in the closing salutation of his letters, an "unprofitable servant."

Gary and I had numerous conversations about marriage over the years, especially when we saw friends and family struggle with its demands and its insistence on selflessness. I used to tease him that he should marry to pass along the family name. He always replied that *that* was the duty of the elder brother, the firstborn son.

It was obvious to Gary and me that healthy marriage requires constant attention and intention. And while we didn't envy the hard work that our married friends had to expend in keeping their vows intact, we did envy them the decisions they do *not* have to make. Their lives seem in some ways to be simpler, more ordered, more predetermined than that of childless, single adults. I can hear some of you *pshaw*-ing me at that statement, but stay with me. The priorities imposed on a married person, at least as we perceived it, are fixed and settled: God, spouse, children, everything else, in that order. The majority of a married person's energy, rightly spent, goes to those primary, inflexible concerns, especially when there are children at home.

The priorities for a single man are considerably more nebulous: God, everything else. Family is still an obligation but in no way the same as that of a wife, husband, or parent.

One of the persistent challenges for Gary and me over the years has been sorting out the "everything else." It usually requires choosing between good and best, which means saying no to a lot of worthwhile invitations, both at and away from home. I don't feel I get it right too often.

I can confidently say, though, that at least once in my life, I did.

When Gary got sick, he became my "everything else," a decision that required no prayer, no deliberation, no weighing of alternatives. My concerns and all my time would center on God and Gary, or maybe better said, on Gary because of God. The wider family, yes, and caring friends, yes, were in that circle too, but they were secondary to my paramount concern for Gary.

For the first time in a long time, maybe the first time ever, my life was about one thing only: how I would serve and care for my brother, how I might embody the love of God to this one saint, each hour, every day.

I will admit, since Gary is not here to make the point for me, that I was far from perfect in my efforts to serve him. Decades of sorting through a host of daily demands was hard for me to unlearn at first. It was, frankly, unsettling to wake up and have so little in the "must do" column of my calendar. But quickly my energy and my attention found their true north. Life took on laser focus.

I've mentioned already that for Gary a life well-lived meant doing small things well over a long period of time. He was heroically unheroic, at peace with his obscure place in a very big picture. This does not mean he didn't want to be impactful. He did, and precisely because he took his small role seriously, he was.

Nor does it suggest that in aiming to please God, Gary didn't care what people thought of him. He valued a good name and knew that the Kingdom of God would be well-served if he could "win the respect of outsiders." He was not obsessed with what others thought of him, but at the same time, he was not oblivious to the fact that his life, like yours and mine, was always in plain view of others. His belief—that faith is personal but not private—made him vigilant to represent Christ honorably in public. Which meant being attentive to details.

Here is an example; it was told to me by one of Gary's close friends:

Gary and a group of guys were at lunch one day when a young woman walked into the restaurant. She was physically striking, obviously aware of that fact, and dressed in a way guaranteed to draw attention to herself. Every man in the room, with varying degrees of subtlety (or lack thereof), studied her from head to toe. Every man in the restaurant could pretty much tell you what every other man's mind was thinking at that moment.

The friend who shared this story with me told me that he very intentionally watched Gary's eyes to see if he would let them go where every other man's were going. It would almost seem freakish for Gary to resist so small a temptation. But Gary did. He *noticed* the woman but controlled his eyes and, ostensibly, his thoughts. And don't think for an instant that this came easily to Gary. He was a hot-blooded man like any other, but had prayed for purity of thought, had trained his eyes, and had cultivated a mindset that allowed him to see and honor and love women without objectifying them. In other words, to treat them as Christ would.

This depth of discipline might seem extreme or prudish, but it reflects the devotion Gary brought to his daily life. The fellow who shared this story with me knew Gary well and for many years. He said that that one small incident spoke to him more convincingly about the reality of Gary's faith than anything else he ever saw in Gary's life.

There's a song I wrote that, for me, captures the life Gary lived.

> *I did not save the world today,*
> *Or change the course of history,*
> *I walked the small and quiet way,*
> *The life that God has given me.*
>
> *I woke up with the morning sun,*
> *I sat awhile to think and pray,*
> *I did my work till the day was done,*
> *But I did not save the world today.*
>
> *I tried to live with gratitude,*
> *To do the good that I could do,*
> *To love the people close to me,*
> *My neighbors and my family,*

To share the kindness I've been shown,
To trust the Love that is my home,
To celebrate the tiny part I play,
But I did not save the world today.

I hear the politicians speak,
Such big ideas and lofty claims,
My life, to theirs, seems small and weak,
But in God's big hand we weigh the same.

The saints and poets seem to know,
The law behind the ocean tide,
The world gets changed and moved along,
By little gestures multiplied.

So I try to live with gratitude,
To do the good that I can do,
To love the people close to me,
My neighbors and my family,
To share the kindness I've been shown,
To trust the Love that is my home,
To celebrate the tiny part I play,
But I did not save the world today.

DURING GARY'S FINAL SPRING, I jotted down some thoughts about what I was learning from my role as a caregiver:

Today marks nine months since Gary was diagnosed with inoperable brain cancer. Based on the initial diagnosis and a seemingly precipitous decline early on, I don't think any of us expected that he would still be with us now. But he is, and his family and friends are deeply grateful for the lighthearted, hopeful, loving presence that he continues to be.

The time at home has given me occasion, and at times has forced me, to sit and reflect. And some of that reflection has lead to what, at present, is an ongoing but incomplete conversation I'm having with myself.

It struck me recently that there has been a common theme, even if only implied, in many of the books I've read in the past two or three years. The idea seems to go something like this: We are all, as never before, members of a "global community." Information about everything everywhere all the time is readily available to us via the internet. There are significant, very real challenges in the world today—hunger, war, lack of clean water, human trafficking and slavery, environmental concerns, and so forth—challenges about which we can be thoroughly informed and toward which we, the church in particular, should be marshaling a vigorous, concerted effort. The books encourage us, sometimes overtly and sometimes by suggestion, to take heroic steps to address the problems, to do things that are visible, newsworthy, and significant. Words like reckless, radical, passionate, extreme, and crazy seem to be the new template for what constitutes a genuinely worthwhile Christian, biblically oriented life. Big solutions to big problems.

Before I go further, let me say that I've been challenged, gratefully and deeply so, by the books I have in mind. They are thought-provoking and beneficially irritating to me. And I believe that those who know and love and seek to follow Christ should be passionate (without being ostentatious), will be radical (but not always in visible ways and rarely because they set out to be), and may be deemed reckless or crazy (by those who don't ascribe to the kingdom ethic). And I wholeheartedly agree that it is part of the church's mission, not just now but since the start, to be a voice, maybe *the* voice, for a compassionate and civil society.

But I make this confession: As I've read those books, I have found myself asking, as if faith were some kind of competitive sport, whether I am radical enough, or reckless or crazy or passionate or extreme enough, to qualify as a *bona fide* disciple of Christ. The question usually leads to mild embarrassment, or worse—contempt and ingratitude— for the quiet life I lead in a small, rural town. *If I were a better Christian, I would be doing momentous and dangerous and newsworthy things. Perhaps I need to go far away, or move to the inner city, or do something worthy of a book.* The weight of those thoughts is hardly encouraging or productive. And perhaps my confession reveals what an insecure, self-conscious, legalistic soul I can be.

Some, of course, *are* called to bring down fire from heaven and slay giants and walk on water, and they are given courage and skill adequate to those tasks. But most of us, or so it appears to me, are called to live lives that are hardly heroic in the traditional sense of the word. Instead of courage for a short season, we are given perseverance for a long one. Rather than white-hot passion, we are given devotion that burns with a slow, steady flame. In place of a moment's enthusiasm about an urgent cause of the day, we are given a quietly persistent commitment to the comprehensive work of knowing Christ and making Him known.

Increasingly, I am convinced that the Kingdom of God moves forward most enduringly when ordinary people do small things kindly and well over a long period of time.

Oswald Chambers, after noting that Peter found it relatively easy to walk on water for a few seconds, but difficult to follow Jesus on dry land week after week, wrote that "it [requires] the supernatural grace of God to live twenty-four hours in every day as a saint, to go through the drudgery as a disciple, to live an ordinary, unobserved, ignored existence as a disciple of Jesus. It is inbred in us that we have to do exceptional things for God, but we have not. We have [only] to be exceptional in the ordinary things, to be holy in mean streets, [and to be loving] among mean people."[33]

The cancer season has been a sobering lesson in being small. And yet, in the midst of it, I have sensed the quiet, humble, liberating invitation to an unheroic life. Liberating because it might just free me to genuinely love people—individual souls up close rather than big causes from a distance—and emancipate me from a slavish dependence on the praise and attention of others for some sense of validation.

The vocabulary for my present season of life is hardly glamorous. Passionate, extreme, crazy, radical—those words don't fit very well. Tedious, confined, tired, unnoticed (but also, joyful, restful, real)—those are the words that more honestly describe the landscape of my life these days. And unless I am sadly mistaken, those same words might well apply to the most significant of our human endeavors and to the most valued of human relationships.

What, after all, are marriage and parenting but the unheroic call to lives of daily self-denial and attentiveness to the needs of others? What are they but a million small decisions made over a lifetime to view one's life in reference to family, in hopes that our loved ones will know the presence and blessing of God? It seems to me, from the outside looking in, that the love of spouse for spouse, or that of parent for child, can be, at times and often for long seasons, draining and unrewarded and, heaven forbid, unfulfilling. It is hard, unheroic work, but it is also irreplaceable. What kind of world will it be if the humbling work of making family is altogether lost to our insistent call for individual happiness and self-fulfillment?

And what is friendship, rightly lived, but the unheroic call to a thousand small conversations, countless prayers, and a myriad of encouraging words from one person to another over a lifetime? What is it but the bearing of burdens, the sharing of gifts, the asking of uncomfortable questions, and the possible discomfort of necessary confrontation?

What is citizenship but the unheroic call to dwell in a fallen world with an awareness that every small, infinitesimal life, lived with integrity or not, has potential bearing on every other small, infinitesimal life in the body politic? What is it but the call to work ethically in the marketplace and on the land, to be wise and generous stewards of whatever wealth God entrusts to us, and to live with kindness, compassion, and integrity toward others?

Please don't misunderstand me. I am grateful for the heroic and inspiring among us. And I am very aware that all followers of Christ, heroic or not, are to be lights on a hill, to do good however they can, and to be courageous witnesses to truth. But maybe the way we best do all of those things is by accepting at the outset that our call is to be servants, not heroes; to be storytellers and not necessarily story subjects; and to decrease so that Christ might increase.

My brother's role at present is to be sick. My role at present is to be present. His is to be weak and forgetful. Mine is to be available and remembering. His is to be needy. Mine is to serve. For both of us, our role is to be brothers, to be friends, to be alive, to show forth the love of God however we can. It is small stuff. But it is the only stuff that matters, whether anyone else sees it or not. The One who needs to see it does see and does validate its acceptability. Otherwise, at such a time as this, how could we possibly be so thankful, laugh so deeply, or sense such gladness in the very midst of it all?

Summer

GARY'S CONDITION CONTINUED TO decline during the spring-time. As summer approached, I posted the following message on my website:

> Following Gary's MRI a week ago, we received the unhappy but not unexpected news that his tumor shows "significant progression." You might recall that, for about six months, the tumor has been stable and has shown no signs of growth. We had been told all along, though, that the tumor was very much alive—merely napping—and in all medical probability, it would awaken at some point and begin to grow again, maybe aggressively. The past couple of weeks, during which Gary has been increasingly tired, weak, and confused, have given us reason to expect that things have taken a turn

for the worse. Walking has been very difficult for him—impossible without assistance—and he is sleeping for many or most hours of the day. His eyes have lost something of their light, he does not laugh or smile quite so readily as he has in the past few months, and it is hard to engage him conversationally. He is still pleasant, always appreciative, and totally trusting, but we cannot deny that he is trickling away from us, and barring a miraculous healing from God, he seems to be in the homestretch of his race. It is sad and hard to watch, but we remind ourselves that our assignment as a family is now what it has been all along—to love him, and one another, as best we can for whatever time we're given. It is a privilege and a gift to be at this place.

A couple of days ago, a close friend of Gary's, whose wife has esophageal cancer, came by to visit. For most of that day and for the entirety of that visit, Gary communicated merely with head nods and single syllable replies. As the visit was drawing to a close, I asked Gary if he'd say a prayer. He bowed his head, reclaimed his native tongue, and with total clarity and in complete sentences offered an eloquent and grateful prayer for his friends. He ended his prayer with the same words I've heard him speak hundreds of times before, "Lord Jesus, we love You, but we pray for grace every day to love You more."

Even in his weakness, Gary teaches me how to live.

I played at a gathering in Atlanta last night, one of the rare times I've left home in the past nine and a half months. Before I left, I kissed Gary goodbye and went through a sweet ritual that I usually reserve till bedtime:

"I love you," I say.

"I love *you*," he says.

"I'm glad you're my brother," I say.

"I'm glad you're *my* brother," he says.

"You're the best brother in the world," I say.

"*You're* the best brother in the world," he says.

We've been sharing those words, or ones like them, for many, many years. Somehow they feel different now. And they are the ones that matter most.

BY JUNE, HOSPICE NURSES became regular visitors to the house. Gary could sometimes sit up in bed, with help, but spent most of his days quietly resting.

These were my thoughts on June 30:

By any measure, Isaiah 55 is one of the richest passages in Holy Scripture. The ancient Jewish prophet writes with profundity about the nature of God, with humility about the smallness of man, with urgency about Israel's idolatry, and with glad expectation about the future. He also addresses the curious, inscrutable, sometimes hurtful ways of God:

"For my thoughts are not your thoughts,
neither are your ways my ways,"
declares the LORD.
"As the heavens are higher than the earth,
so are my ways higher than your ways
and my thoughts than your thoughts."
—Isaiah 55:8–9 NIV

The older I get, and the more I see, the more I find myself leaning on those words, not so much for comfort, not because they explain anything, but rather to be reminded that human wisdom is at best a dim light in a dense forest on a dark night.

The fifty-fifth chapter of Isaiah concludes with a scene of pure goodness, with an eruption of life and restoration, with a sunburst of triumphant hope. It is a benediction, a promise, a happily ever and ever and ever after.

Fifty-five.

Today is Gary's birthday. His fifty-fifth. Isaiah's words, while always appropriate to where we are in life, seem ideally suited for our family on today's occasion. We continue to walk through a season which requires us to trust that the head-scratching ways of God are not just higher, but better than we could ever imagine, and that the day of the hand-clapping trees is the reality for which we are destined.

One might suggest that there are three birthdays that matter most in life.

There is of course the first one—physical birth—the one that brings us into the world, bundles of "great and mysterious opportunity,"[34] screaming for all we're worth until the air of the world fills our lungs and we set out on the path to life that is truly life.

The second—spiritual birth—is when we surrender to the wise counsel of Isaiah, who foresaw the coming of Christ and admonished the people then and now to:

> Seek the LORD while he may be found;
> call on him while he is near.
> Let the wicked forsake their ways
> and the unrighteous their thoughts.
> Let him turn to the LORD, and he will have
>   mercy on him,
> and to our God, for he will freely pardon.
> —Isaiah 55:6–7 NIV

The third birthday, if it can be called such, occurs when we end our time in the less-than-pristine air of this world and begin to breathe the clean air of heaven.

Gary was somewhat alert this morning. When I told him it was his birthday, his eyebrows arched upward, his eyes opened with interest, and he said, "Really?" That may have been his longest sentence of the day. He enjoyed a celebratory breakfast—strong black coffee and hot Krispy Kreme donuts—before sleeping through most of the day. And now, as the sun sets after a hot June 30, niece Mary Katherine and I are posted on both sides of Gary's bed, Sam and Charlie (the dogs) are stretched out at our feet, and the newest fifty-five-year-old member of our family is fast asleep.

We are grateful for another year with Gary.

And for another day.

He has had the first birthday.

And the second.

Now he and we await the third, hopeful that in deeper ways than we can imagine, we will "eat what is good and . . . delight in the richest of fare."[35]

Talk

On July 18, a clear hot day, the house was pleasantly full of family, enough so that I could go outside to do some physical work, something I enjoy and that I knew would be good for my mind. Nephew Caleb and I were trimming trees on Gary's side, the west side, of the pond when I got a call, midmorning, to come back to the house. Ann needed to speak with me.

Ann, a high school classmate of mine and now a hospice nurse, had become like family to us over the months. From the start, it was obvious that she was not a mere hireling. If workers in her position are supposed to be detached, emotionally uninvolved, professionally distant, and clinical, she failed miserably at her job. And we are thankful. We appreciated that she brought her heart and her tears to work and allowed them to be part of the caring process—a sure sign of God's kindness to us.

When I returned to the house, she and I sat on the porch, not far away from Gary's bed. He was asleep. With little explanation—and tenderness appropriate to the moment—she told me it was time for us to stop feeding Gary. His appetite had declined. Eating was difficult. It was obvious, and had been for months, that Gary was not beating the cancer. His body was, to use the medical terminology, "actively dying"—feverish, fatigued, feeble—and we should not interfere with that process. Hearing those words and facing the reality of Gary's eminent death was gut-wrenching, as much as the words of the July morning a year past that had started us on the cancer season.

"His body is telling us that it is time to die. We need to let that happen."

I understood, of course; we all did. But willfully withholding food from Gary, day after day, would be a difficult compassion to put into practice. There seemed a coldness, even a brutality, to denying him basic sustenance. And Ann's explanation, that his body did not really hunger for food any longer, hardly made the assignment easier.

We trusted her training and experience—even more so, her love for our family—and we did as we were told, but not without anguish.

The mother who had fed him as a baby, a boy, a man—the woman whose life had been spent in large part over a stove feeding armies of appetites—did the nearly unthinkable. No food.

The brothers, the sisters, the father—all of whom in recent months had prepared meals, fed Gary by the spoonful, given him drink, tried to gladden him with things he liked to eat—accepted that in a very short while, his body, once so strong, so alive and life-giving, so radiant with joy and good humor, would sleep in death.

There was a jolting finality to the "do not feed" decision. Though we had continued to pray, selfishly perhaps, for Gary's healing, this day had been foreseeable. When the probable became all but certain that morning, when I looked across the room at my brother who would sleep for a few more days and then be gone from us forever, a sadness, a sorrow, a powerlessness that had previously only been hinted at became sickeningly undeniable.

Without knowing exactly how we might care for him during those last few days, we continued—you would have been so proud of your family—to serve, to reach out to, to love our dear Gary. We could not feed him physically, but all of us, without saying so, sensed that in very fundamental ways, he was still fully alive and capable of feeling the affections of this world even as he prepared for the affections of the one ahead.

Ann told us that Gary might live for another week or so.

BY THAT SATURDAY, JULY 21, we all carried with us, alone and together, the knowledge that Gary might pass at any moment. It's fair to say that we hovered at his bedside. There was little we could do, but we all wanted to be there as close and as long as possible.

Months previous, when Gary had been alert and reasonably clear-thinking, we had all spoken the things that needed to be spoken—the thanks, the hopes, the affections. I told Gary, countless times, as he had me, how grateful I was to have him as my brother, how endlessly proud of him I was, how I would try to follow his example in loving Christ and serving people. There are some things a body simply can't repeat too often or make too clear.

That last afternoon, I found myself alone with Gary. I know now that Linda had emptied the porch so I might have some time with him undisturbed.

As I had become accustomed to doing, I was sitting on Gary's right side, with the bed rail down, holding his hand and leaning in so that my face was close to his.

I told Gary once again the things I most wanted him to know, taking solace in the medical assertion that hearing is the last sense to leave us. I hoped he could hear me. I hoped he could understand.

I would have given anything for Gary to be able to speak to me, to say some final words. But for days now, he had been virtually speechless. If he *had* been able to talk to me one last time that day, I have no doubt what he would have told me.

And so, I spoke *for* him, out loud, in his hearing:

"Gary, I know you can't talk anymore. But I think I know what you'd say to me if you could. You've already said it lots of times, but I think you'd want to say it again. You'd thank me for taking such good care of you since you've been sick."

With that, Gary's eyes, already closed as they had been for most of the recent days, clinched tightly in recognition and affirmation of what I'd said.

"You would tell me that I am the best brother in the world. You'd tell me that I've been your best friend and that you're thankful that God let us be brothers."

His face was fully engaged. *Yes, yes, yes! That's what I'd say if I could.*

"You'd tell me to love Christ, to serve Him, to live for Him. And I will, Bah. You'd remind me that we'll be together again, that this is not the end.

"Mostly, you'd tell me that you love me. And, Bah, I love you, and I'm so glad you're my brother.

"Don't be afraid, Gary. You can go now. You've run your race well. You finished good. We'll be okay. You can go home. We'll miss you so much, but we won't be far behind you."

At that point, I might have prayed. Maybe I tried to sing one last time. I really don't recall.

It was my last conversation with Gary.

How many times since then have I wished I could have just one more?

Later that night, he was gone.

Wedding

A MESSAGE TO FRIENDS, July 22, 2012:

We have wondered for some time now, weeks at least, what Gary is capable of seeing. From the outset of his cancer season, we've known that the brain tumor was compromising his eyesight. But we have had reason to believe, even these last several hours, that he has some vision left.

This evening, after a long, hard, sweet, sad day of decline in Gary's condition, we pulled up the shades of the westward facing porch so we could watch a Harris County sunset together. From where we sat, the green pastures, the still waters of our pond, the trees in full foliage, and the house that Gary lived in before he became ill were visible.

Gary's eyes were sleepy but open, and the evening light was strong. We think Gary saw the sunset. If he did, it was his last in this world.

And we can only imagine what sort of sunrise greets him this morning.

Gary Carlton Levi, born June 30, 1957, went home—to his true home with Christ—shortly after midnight, July 22, 2012, a day prior to the one-year anniversary of his brain tumor diagnosis. He died at the farm, surrounded by ones who knew him best and loved him most—Dad, Mom, Beth (with Greg and Aron), Linda (with Kevan), Laura, and me. We were close beside him, assuring him that we would be here till the end and letting him know that we love him enough to gladly let him go when God calls him. After a few labored breaths, he became quiet and slipped away from us.

Of course, our hearts break. The world already seems strangely diminished without Gary in it, but we are hopeful and grateful just the same. Having spent this year with him and with one another—in a room where death was so obviously present—we will never look at this world quite the same. Something momentous has been taken from it. And none of us will ever think of heaven the same. It will forever be the place, going forward, where we will find our dear brother and son again.

Someone suggested last night that, as Gary approached his end in this world, I was standing beside him as his best man, helping him prepare for his wedding day. It has arrived. Gary was ready.

"Who gives this man to be married to the Maker of the Mountains?"

"I do, dear Lord. I do."

Shovel

THREE DECADES AGO, DAD moved a small white chapel from Suggsville, Alabama, near Mobile, to the northeast corner of the pasture at the farm. His maternal ancestors had been members of the congregation that first met in that chapel when it was built in 1806. Dad had recently come to Christ, the last in our family to do so, and wanted to build something on the property that was a visible expression of his and the family's faith in God. He also wanted it to be a place in which we, the family, might celebrate special occasions.

Over the years, it has been the place that Dad had hoped it might be for us, but it has also been the site of weddings, celebrations, concerts, and assorted other events for our friends and community.

A few years ago, long before Gary got sick, Dad told us that he'd like to be buried there. An antique wrought-iron fence—I'm not sure where it came from—was placed around a twenty-five-foot by twenty-five-foot square section of ground on the east side of the chapel.

A FEW WEEKS BEFORE Gary passed away—on a pleasant, almost cool Saturday summer morning—twenty-five or so men from the weekly front-porch gathering came together at the chapel to perform a peculiar kindness. They were there at the invitation, and with the blessing, of our family.

They assembled just after sunrise, shovels in hand, to cut a hole in the dense but, thankfully, rain-soaked Georgia clay. They had come to prepare the place where Gary's body would be laid to rest.

They worked in pairs, each twosome digging enough soil to fill a wheelbarrow and then pushing it away to make room for the next team—assembly-line gravediggers if you will. There was laughter and conversation. There was perspiration and deep breath. There were tears. There was gladness and a deep sense of purpose to the morning's labor.

I was fortunate to be with them.

Before the digging began, we gathered inside the chapel to pray and talk about the task before us. It was agreed that our labor that day would demonstrate three things: an act of affection, an act of community, and an act of defiance.

An act of affection: a visible, practical gift to our family, as if to say, "Someone, at some point in the near future, is going to have to do this difficult thing. We'd like to do it because we can do it with a love and with a purpose that no hired hand could possibly bring to the task. We have so wanted to prove ourselves useful to you over the past months. Let our hands be the ones that break this ground."

All of those present that morning knew and loved Gary. Most had known him for years. All had benefited from his influence in their lives. Some were his "children in the faith." When they first heard the news of his illness, these same men had wept unashamedly, prayed fervently, and spoken unreservedly about their indebtedness to Gary. And on that Saturday morning, while believing in the miraculous but resigned to the likely, they dirtied their hands and feet to prepare a place for his body. And a mighty fine place it was when all was said and done, precise and orderly and clean, forty inches wide, forty-eight inches deep, ninety-six inches long.

An act of community: Anyone knows that there are easier, quicker, more efficient ways than hand-shoveling to dig a hole in the hard Georgia clay. There are diesel-powered machines that do the work well, for instance. One person on such a machine, impersonal and detached, can get the job done in very little time and with little or no sweat. But these brethren were of the belief that there is something holy about working side by side. And especially for an undertaking like this one, the involvement of the group was an affirmation that the passing of this brother would not be just a private loss but a communal one. There was something sacred about those shovels full of clay.

Lastly, an act of defiance: Someone read a Scripture to start the day:

Since the children have flesh and blood, [Jesus] too shared in their humanity so that by his death he might break the power of him who holds the power of death—that is, the devil—and free those who all their lives were held in slavery by their fear of death.

—Hebrews 2:14–15 NIV

Some, I suppose, might think that ours was a morbid task, one better left to the morticians and their paid crews. For us though, the doing of it allowed us to quietly declare that we will not live as slaves to our fear of dying. Any death, and particularly this one, is unwelcome and unnatural. It still makes us uneasy and afraid, but our work that day was a taunt to the one who would have us live in abject terror of our mortality. We each stood in that grave and thrust our shovels into its heart as if to say, "Death, we will not be afraid of you. Where is your victory? Where is your sting? Have you not heard of Jesus? Have you forgotten His cross? Have you forgotten His empty tomb? Do you think that *we* have forgotten it? Poor death. You poor pitiful thing."

Affection, community, defiance—those ingredients make for a good day. And a good day it was. It reminded each of us that our bodies too will return to the earth by and by.

When Gary was first diagnosed with a brain tumor, and after he agreed to seek medical care, we had to choose, as a family, what kind of treatment he should receive and where. Our options were many, but early on, with Gary's blessing, the decision was made to keep him close to home in the belief that the best medicine—or most preferable death—was that which allowed for the constant nearness of people who knew and loved him. By that decision, we were assured that the last thing Gary would feel, hear, or sense in this world would be the tenderness, reverence, and adoration of those to whom he meant most; in other words, he would leave this world feeling the same things, though to a lesser degree, that he would feel when he took his first breath on the other side.

ON THE EVENING OF the gravedigging, I sent this note to the men:

Saturday evening, June 16, 2012, 9:35 p.m.

Dear Brethren,

Words fail me, but I didn't want the day to end without at least trying to express my thanks to you for your work this morning. How blessed we are, and how heartily can we say with the psalmist, "The boundary lines have fallen for [us] in pleasant places."[36]

I went back to the cemetery this evening by myself. It looked and felt quite different than it did when we were all together there earlier today. This morning there was activity, conversation, and camaraderie. This evening it was stillness, quiet, and solitude. Standing there alone made me grateful that my memories of the place will always include the sight of friends working side by side, the sounds of laughter and lightheartedness, and a sense of belonging that is bigger than any one of us. Knowing that your footprints are in and around the spot where Gary's body will be laid to rest is a comforting thought, and I'm sure he'd be happy to know that you and I had a hand in preparing it.

It is such a gift to follow Christ and to walk through life with men like you. Thank you for sharing your time with me, not just today, but weekly. I am honored, and I am your debtor.

—allen

GARY PASSED AWAY EARLY on a Sunday morning.

On Tuesday of that week, we had a private burial at the farm—just family—and then a public memorial later that afternoon. By day's end, one task remained undone. Gary's casket had been placed in the ground but left uncovered.

Two days later, at 7:00 a.m., just after sunrise, instead of meeting at my house on the porch as we usually did on Thursday mornings, the brethren gathered at the chapel, shovels in hand, to mend the earth and close Gary's grave.

It was a beautiful morning.

We sang a song.
We read and talked about John 21.
We moved the soil back to its place.
We said goodbye.
Our work was done.

Sister

July 27, 2012

Dear Linda, Beth, and Laura,

You, Beth, the last to leave, pulled away from the farm ten minutes ago, and I suppose a new chapter of life officially begins for me—for all of us. Gary is gone. Condolences have been expressed. The body has been buried and the life celebrated. We have stood together, side by side, and done our best at something we felt ill-prepared to do. And at this moment, with the farm sadly quiet all around me, I'm sitting on my porch trying to list, in order of importance, the things I need to do now.

My first task is to tell you how grateful I am to you for loving Gary as you have for all of his fifty-five years, but especially during these past twelve months. He adored you beyond words. His first prayers and deepest affections, even when he was taking Christ to so many others in such far away places, were reserved for us, his family. And I know, because he often told me, how much he loved and delighted in you. He was so proud of you. He knew your faults, as he did mine, but considered them a small thing next to the goodness, the kindness, the generosity, and the graciousness that have made and still make you such a clear reflection of his Lord Jesus. If anyone in this world ever deserved to be loved well and cared for in glowing fashion, it was Gary. That you did so love and care for him, particularly this past year, makes me grateful, and deeply happy for his sake.

I've tried to imagine what he might say if he were writing this letter. I am certain he would begin by encouraging us to press on, to love and honor and tell the story of Christ all our living days. He would remind us of the promises on which we stand and would try to describe, from where he is now, just how glorious is their fulfillment. I can imagine Gary telling us, as he often did with his letters, his calls, his sermons, his very life, "You cannot love Christ too much. You cannot serve Him too fervently. You cannot enjoy Him too deeply. You cannot know Him too well." He would forever and emphatically point us Christ-ward.

But he would also want to express highest praise and deepest thanks to each of you. For the long-running jokes, the good-natured sibling banter, the teasing that only exists among people who are safe in each other's affection, for all the short conversations that left him glad-hearted, he would say thank you.

For the confidence that you placed in him when you called with concerns about the children or marriage or similar weighty matters—a sure sign that you trusted his wisdom, his counsel, and his ability to speak the truth in love—he would say thank you.

For the prayers and encouragement you gave him when he was overseas—the letters, the calls, the pictures, the tangible reminders that he was not forgotten or alone—and for your belief in the rightness of his going into all the nations and making disciples of Jesus, I know that he would say thank you.

For the countless ways you have served him since last July—the mere fact of your presence and your "little, nameless, unremembered acts of kindness and love"[37] that prepared him for heaven—Gary would say, a thousand times, thank you.

For the way you have cared for me, his best friend, at a time when he knew that my heart was breaking, and for his confident hope that I would be equally cared for after he was gone, he would say thank you.

For the prayers—can we ever know their power?—that you have always prayed for him, and for the myriad expressions of generosity you've long since forgotten, Gary would shower you—his friends, his encouragers, his sisters—with thanks and thanks and more thanks. I know he would.

And he would tell you, in capital letters and exclamation points, how much he loves you still. "Loves," rather than "loved," because if the Gospel is true, he is more alive and his love for us is deeper and sweeter and more real today than it has ever been before.

If it is possible to be in heaven and miss the ones we leave behind, Gary might just tell us that he misses us, misses us in a way that causes no sorrow but in a way that admits of an incompleteness until we are all together again. "I miss you," he might say, "but I'm closer to you than you can possibly imagine." In *our* missing there is so much sadness right now. But in Gary's there is perhaps only anticipation and joy for all that we will have when we are reunited. Either way, our sense of absence and separation is rooted in a love for one another, and maybe, as time passes, our missing will grow to be increasingly like his. I hope so.

It is a good thought that the last things Gary experienced in this world—your tenderness and loving regard for him—were but a foreshadowing of what he would encounter on the distant shore. The words that might have greeted him there—"Well done, good and faithful servant"—are words that, at that same moment, could be said of you. As we all enter into our new normal—a world without Gary—I pray that you will do so with the assurance that you did well, very well, in caring for one who, by the end, was "the least of these," weak, weary, needy, and homesick.

Everything around me is thick with Gary's memory just now. It makes me cry, it makes me smile, it makes me glad, it breaks me. But I pray and trust that going forward our individual memories and thoughts of Gary—for we all knew him in our own unique ways—will be a source of great joy to us, and the knowledge that he loved us deeply will be good medicine against the heaviness of the world that he worked so hard to change for the better.

Once we were five.

Now we are four.

I look forward to growing old with you and am here, I promise, if you ever need me.

I love you.

> Empty but full,
> —allen

Anniversary

Dear Bah,

This past weekend I took Jonathan and Andrew to the beach for a couple of days. On the way down, I told them the story of Settalegs and the wild continuous party. They laughed. The story endures, and our useless bit of banter lives on!

Your name, and the memories it evokes, came up often, as it does every day in my thoughts and conversations.

Especially today.

It's been one year. One year since you left us. To those who've assured me that time heals broken hearts, I can only answer "not yet." A host of tears this morning—good, comforting, thankful tears—prove my point. Dad has reminded me a number of times that "we'll get through this, but we won't get over it."

I cannot begin to say how much I miss you. There are moments when realization of your absence doubles me over with a hurt I have no name for. The finality of death and the weight of that awful word "never" (as in, never walk together again, never hear your laughter, never see you across the field—a thousand nevers) force their inflexibility on me a bit more and more every day.

That said, there have been two "nevers," embedded in a promise, that have been a source of great comfort to me since you've been gone: "Never will I leave you; never will I forsake you."

I always did enjoy your presence. I enjoy it still. Sometimes I mistake your absence for one of those long spells when you were far away from home for months or years at a time. I always knew then—as I do now but differently—that there would be reunion. I sometimes wish I could book the flight.

In my prayers this morning—the rainy skies seemed perfectly suited to the day—I asked God, if it be possible and permissible and beneficial, to tell you hello for me, to tell you how much I miss and love you, to tell you that we are well. Did the message reach you? I imagine your face often, alight with that kind aliveness that was always you, and today especially I tried to picture you in that place of no time and no worry. There is a photo on my desk, one taken when we went to Holland, of you standing beside a stream with a field in bloom behind you. The feel of it, the combination of beauty and rest, even the peacefulness of your countenance, strikes me as heavenly. That's how I remember you today.

You are still my favorite company to keep.

Speaking of good company to keep. I have thought today of the many who cared for us, for you, during your sickness. A number of them apparently have the date marked on their calendars and have called or written to let us know that they too remember you fondly.

Dad, Mom, and I had lunch at my house earlier, spoke of things we remember and most miss about you. I think we each struggle with trying to articulate what our lives are like without you here. Your absence is far greater than the sum of its parts. The parts—laughter, teasing, working, dreaming, conversation, even disagreement—can be listed (a long list), but they don't add up to all that we miss. Still, we talked and reminisced gratefully. We sat on my porch and looked over the pastures, which, due to unusual amounts of rain this summer, are deep green and growing in defiance of July.

We went to the chapel and put some flowers—red and white roses—at your grave. We held hands and prayed. We got rained on.

One year.

I tell people, to their obvious surprise, that the year you and I shared with cancer was the best year of my life. Difficult and hurtful, yes. But by any measure that really matters—depth of purpose, intensity of focus, freedom from triviality, honesty of affection, genuineness of love and joy and peace, reliance on and trust in God—it was "The Year" for me. To be with my favorite person every day, to relive so much shared history, and to be free from the petty cares that so often clutter my life added up to something for which I can find no words. I wish, of course, that I'd never experienced it, especially knowing how difficult it was for you, but I'm grateful.

And in recalling it today—that last sweet mile with its uninvited joy and unexpected grace—I do so with a prayer that God will keep me at the place where I was when every day was about one thing—loving the weak (you) and trusting the strong (Him).

Enough for now. Surely I can be forgiven of this curious compulsion to write you a letter today. It brings a comforting sense of your presence, gives voice to my sadness, and allows me to revisit the ancient paths that make me tenaciously hopeful on this anniversary. If it could be done without upsetting the perfect peace of heaven, I like to imagine that somehow our words, our prayers, the love of many rose up to meet you today.

I'm really tired, and it's time for bed.

I love you, Bah.

I'm glad you're my brother.

You're the best brother in the world.

Still and forever,
—allen

Close

HE WAS WALKING UP the staircase inside the big house. Had on a baseball cap. He didn't say anything, but it was him. And then it was over.

That's the only dream I've had of Gary since he died. It constitutes the complete but meager reply that I have received thus far to my specific prayer for dreams about my brother. I wish God would give me more, but I don't think that in withholding them He is being tight-fisted or unkind.

For now, I find Gary in other places, in places more concrete than dreams.

Around a table at a gathering of friends.

In a hundred "good mornings" at a schoolhouse door.

Whenever I sing a song and tell a story.

In the unheroic life of secret generosity and radiant goodness.

Gary is always there somehow.

One day, perhaps, I'll be too tired or too feeble to look for Gary in the places I find him now. Maybe then I'll be given dreams. The kind that are vivid and long and beckoning.

And after the dreams, the Reality—as indescribable in its sublimity as Afghanistan is in its austerity.

IN A HUNDRED YEARS, Gary will be entirely forgotten among men, just as you and I will be. At some point between now and then, someone will say his name, not knowing that it will be the final time the words "Gary Levi" will ever be spoken on this planet in reference to the one we know and love. Those who see his name on the headstone beside the chapel will likely take more interest in the other words inscribed there—"perhaps today"—than in the eight gilded letters that identify him. That's okay; his name, his new name, will endure.

That said, I trust we will try to keep his memory alive for one another, for as long as we can.

I will do my part.

When you come to the farm, I will show you the little bench he built in the woods, his secret place to sit and pray and listen.

I can take you to the place where he and I built bluebird houses during the year he was sick, the same bluebird houses you see now along the fence lines and in the pastures.

I will take you to the scene of the first Drunkard's Dance.

And to the backyard that was home to his entire, short-lived javelin career.

I can take you to the high school and show you the exact place he stood by the back door each morning.

I can take you to the site of the sawmill where we concocted the story of Mac's plastic cheek, and to the barn where Robert encountered the flying scalyback.

We can lay on the floor at my house, look up at the underside of my dining room table, and read the inscription he burned into the wood for me.

I will show you your name in his prayer book.

I can take you to where I was standing when I first got the news that changed everything.

And to the very place where the little boy with the fedora and the crooked buttons was standing when he smiled for the camera.

At each place, I'm sure I'll think of something new to tell you about him.

And, painful though it might be, we can revisit the bittersweet year of our long farewell with Gary, those last tender days of the long ride home.

Having you beside me, reliving all those moments, will be better than dreams.

Better by far.

I'LL CLOSE NOW.

I fear I have lived up to my initial expectation that, at best, I have rendered a woefully incomplete portrait of Gary. But I send these words on their way with hopes they will find a good home somewhere. If in reading them, you have smiled or laughed or felt thankful or owned your sadness or wished you could have known Gary better, then I am satisfied that my effort was not in vain.

I look forward to our ongoing reminiscences about Gary. I want to hear again what you love and what you miss about him. I want to know the things you'll tell your children, and theirs, about him.

And don't be surprised if someday we are riding down the road, not talking for a long stretch, and right out of the blue I turn to you and ask, "Bah,"—long pause—". . . whatcha' reckon Settalegs is doing right now?"

The best is yet to come.

—allen

Notes

1. Words and music by Allen Levi, *Bigger Picture*, "Everyday There is Something." Copyright © 2008 by Allen Levi.

2. Words and music by Allen Levi, unrecorded, "Never More Alive." Copyright © 2015 by Allen Levi.

3. Romans 12:13 NIV

4. Acts 9:36–39 NIV

5. Ephesians 5:1–2 NIV

6. Words by Henry Van Dyke, music by Wolfgang Beethoven, "Joyful, Joyful, We Adore Thee."

7. Words and music by Allen Levi, unrecorded, "Sing A Song, Tell A Story." Copyright © 2015 by Allen Levi.

8. "[Beauty] arrives through a sustained and adorational attentiveness to all that we encounter..." Eugene Peterson, *The Jesus Way: A Conversation on the Ways That Jesus Is the Way*, (Grand Rapids, Mich.: Eerdmans, 2007), 181.

9. 1 Corinthians 1:27 KJV

10. 1 Corinthians 8:1 ISV

11. Ecclesiastes 1:18 NIV

12. Job 14:1 NIV

13. Isaiah 53:3 KJV

14. C. S. Lewis, *Mere Christianity* (San Francisco: HarperSan-Francisco, 2001).

15. Jeremiah 6:14 NIV

16. Words and music by Allen Levi, *We Have Seen Him* (2009), "World Where He's a Stranger." Copyright © 2009 by Allen Levi

16. John 16:33 NIV

17. Psalm 32:1 NIV

18. Matthew 5:4 NIV

19. Matthew 5:8 NIV

20. C. S. Lewis, *Mere Christianity* (San Francisco: HarperSan-Francisco, 2001).

21. C. Soanes, *Concise Oxford English Dictionary*, 11th ed. (New York: Oxford University Press, 2004).

22. Acts 10:38 NIV

23. John 13:15 NIV

24. 1 John 3:18 NIV

25. Titus 2:14 NIV

26. Psalm 84:10 NIV

27. Romans 8:28 NIV

28. Romans 5:3–4 NIV

29. Ted Loder, *Guerrillas of Grace* (San Diego: Lura-Media, 1984).

30. G. K. Chesterton, *What's Wrong with the World* (New York: Dodd, Mead and Company, 1910).

31. Zechariah 9:12 NIV

32. Oswald Chambers and James Reimann, *My Utmost for His Highest: An Updated Edition in Today's Language: The Golden Book of Oswald Chambers* (Grand Rapids, Mich.: Discovery House, 1992).

33. John Baillie, *A Diary of Private Prayer* (New York: Charles Scribner's Sons, 1949).

34. Isaiah 55:2 NIV

35. Psalm 16:6 NIV

36. Wordsworth, "Tintern Abbey," stanza II.

A number of items referred to in this book—the Story of Two Brothers, Doorkeeper's Prayer, specific photographs, and others—can be viewed or heard by visiting the "Gary" tab at www.AllenLevi.com.

MORE FROM ALLEN LEVI

MUSIC

COCKBURN STREET (1992)

BEYOND THE SHELL (1994)

LOVE LOOKING DOWN (1994)

OPEN WINDOWS (1995)

TALKING WITH TYLER (1996)

RIVERTOWN (1996)

WE HAVE SEEN HIM (1997)

LIBERTY (1997)

LEARNING HOW TO SEE (1997)

JOY (WITH ED CASH AND BEBO NORMAN) (1997)

ACCIDENTAL ROADS (1998)

OLD DOGS, NEW TRICKS (1999)

CHANGE FOR THE BETTER (2000)

BEFORE THE COUNT OF THREE (2000)

THE MOON IS ROUND (2002)

TAP THE KALEIDOSCOPE (2003)

LIVE (2003)

PEOPLE IN MY TOWN (2006)

BIGGER PICTURE (2008)

FAVORITES (2010)

LOVE IS SOMETHING THAT WE LEARN (2010)

FAITH OF A FARMER (2014)

Available www.AllenLevi.com, store.RabbitRoom.com,
iTunes, and wherever great music is sold.

ALSO FROM RABBIT ROOM PRESS

EVERLASTING IS THE PAST
by Walter Wangerin Jr.

THE WORLD ACCORDING TO NARNIA
by Jonathan Rogers

REAL LOVE FOR REAL LIFE
by Andi Ashworth

BEHOLD THE LAMB OF GOD: *An Advent Narrative*
by Russ Ramsey

THE MOLEHILL: *An Annual Literary Collection*

THE WINGFEATHER SAGA
by Andrew Peterson

THE WILDERKING TRILOGY
by Jonathan Rogers

FIN'S REVOLUTION
by A. S. Peterson

Available at RabbitRoom.com and wherever great books are sold.

RABBIT ROOM
— P R E S S —
Nashville, Tennessee

www.RabbitRoom.com
www.AllenLevi.com